HOLY
BLASPHEMIES

HOLY BLASPHEMIES

God, Mystery, and the Spiritual

Thomas P. Rausch, SJ

Paulist Press
New York / Mahwah, NJ

Cover image by BGStock72/Shutterstock.com
Cover design by Sharyn Banks
Book design by Lynn Else

Library of Congress Cataloging-in-Publication Data
Names: Rausch, Thomas P., author.
Title: Holy blasphemies : God, mystery, and the spiritual / Thomas P. Rausch, SJ.
Description: New York/Mahwah, NJ : Paulist Press, [2023] | Summary: "Reflections on God, creation, life, the Christian mysteries from the perspective of theology and spirituality"—Provided by publisher.
Identifiers: LCCN 2022042416 (print) | LCCN 2022042417 (ebook) | ISBN 9780809156467 (paperback) | ISBN 9780809188079 (ebook)
Subjects: LCSH: Christianity. | Theology. | Creation. | Jesus Christ—Person and offices. | Prayer—Christianity. | Christian life—Study and teaching.
Classification: LCC BR121.3 .R385 2023 (print) | LCC BR121.3 (ebook) | DDC 230/.2—dc23/eng/20221214
LC record available at https://lccn.loc.gov/2022042416
LC ebook record available at https://lccn.loc.gov/2022042417

ISBN 978-0-8091-5646-7 (paperback)
ISBN 978-0-8091-8807-9 (e-book)

Published by Paulist Press
997 Macarthur Boulevard
Mahwah, New Jersey 07430
www.paulistpress.com

Printed and bound in the
United States of America

For Pope Francis

The human person grows more, matures more and is sanctified more to the extent that he or she enters into relationships, going out from themselves to live in communion with God, with others and with all creatures. In this way, they make their own that trinitarian dynamism which God imprinted in them when they were created.

Pope Francis, *Laudato si'* 240

CONTENTS

CONTENTS

ACKNOWLEDGMENTS

AFTER FIFTY YEARS as a priest and more than forty years of teaching, mostly undergraduates, I long for a new language to present the good news of the gospel as I continue to ask: How can we help others to become more aware of the mystery of God's loving presence in our lives? We all have many questions. This book is an effort to address some of those questions that many ask or simply dismiss with a negative response.

Much of what is presented here flows out of those years in the classroom. Also included are stories from homilies reflected on and developed, reaching out to those hungry for some transforming experiences of faith, words that enlighten, or stories that touch them personally. Some chapters are taken from talks prepared for retreats, among them two for retired priests, wonderful men after years of ministry now experiencing the diminishments of their seniority. I have learned as much as I've shared, discovering God's goodness in unexpected places, in awe before the beauty of creation, reflected in the words of Scripture, learning to live with ambiguity and difference.

I will draw especially on the teachings of Pope Francis in his programmatic apostolic exhortation *Evangelii gaudium*, "The Joy of the Gospel" (2013); his response to the two-year Synod of Bishops on the Family (2014–2015), the post-synodal apostolic exhortation, *Amoris laetitia*, "The Joy of Love" (2016); his encyclical on the protection of the earth, *Laudato si'* (2015); and another encyclical, *Fratelli tutti* (2020), reminding us that we belong to one human family.

Many friends encountered along the way have also contributed to what appears in this book. I am especially indebted to my old friend and colleague Michael Downey for his careful review of the manuscript and always insightful suggestions. And to Paul McMahon at Paulist Press for his sensitive editorial work. And to all my friends at Saint Lawrence Church in Redondo Beach, California, who have long been encouraging. To all these I am most grateful.

INTRODUCTION

W E NO LONGER LIVE in a culture that supports our faith. Post-Enlightenment thinking is decidedly secular. Our Western culture has been "disenchanted," stripped of its mystery and banishing the transcendent. It is too often centered not on God and God's grace but on the self. What is not demonstrable or able to be personally experienced is not real. Surveys track the increasing number of church members who "disaffiliate." Young people continue to be numbered among the "nones," those who, when asked about their religious tradition, answer "none."

The Christian metanarrative, as postmodern scholars would call it, tells us how God, the Creator of the heavens and the earth, sent his only beloved Son Jesus into the world to save us from our sins. After a brief public ministry, he accomplished our salvation by his death on the cross. On the third day he rose again. Appearing to his own, the first witnesses, he poured out on them the Holy Spirit, establishing his Church, sending his apostles and disciples out to teach and to baptize in the name of the Father, the Son, and the Holy Spirit. The Church endures to this day, calling men and women to new life in the Spirit, the forgiveness of their sins, offering the gift of everlasting life. The Apostles' Creed, a confession of faith from the ancient church of Rome, is a summary of this story. This is what most Christians believe.

Yet sometimes in quiet moments I have certain misgivings; I continue to wonder and raise questions: Is all this true? Is God real? How can I grasp the very idea of a God who simply IS, without beginning or end? Is there a divine presence in a universe that often seems cold and impersonal? Does God care? Why do so many suffer so much? Why doesn't the divine presence reveal itself more clearly?

Could not God have found a better, more obvious way to communicate with us, to share something of his mystery? Even the disciples of Jesus seem to have struggled with this; the Gospels tell us that one of them asked: How is it that you will reveal yourself to us and not to the world (John 14:22)?

Many Catholics today would have a difficult time answering these and other questions: Who is Jesus, what did he teach, why do we need to be "saved," and what does salvation mean? Others ask, Why did Jesus have to die? What kind of God would require the death of his beloved Son? Can we really believe that the bread and wine become the body and blood of Jesus Christ? And why do we need the Church anyway?

True, the Jesus movement has left its mark on history and even changed it. Christianity has long been the world's largest religion, though it has recently been surpassed by Islam. But too often the sins of Christians and even of churches are more striking than the message their mission is to proclaim. Many are turned off by religion, scandalized. It is sometimes difficult to fault them.

From the beginning, the Christian movement was missionary. But after the so-called discovery of the new world in the fifteenth and sixteenth centuries—the vast continents of Africa, Asia, and the Americas with their millions of inhabitants—the Church launched a great missionary movement down to the Second Vatican Council. Driven by the belief that those without baptism would be irretrievably lost, members of religious orders planted the Church on these continents, often at considerable expense on both sides and with many martyrs.

The Catholic Church long held to the ancient principle *extra ecclesia, nulla salus*, "no salvation outside the Church," first formulated by the third-century bishop Cyprian of Carthage. But another tradition traces back to Aquinas, who seems to have held that the universality of God's salvific will allowed for an ignorance of Christ that was not culpable. An awareness of the multitudes of peoples from the new worlds, apparently excluded from God's grace, moved Dominican theologians in Spain and Jesuits in Rome to begin reflecting on that tradition. They spoke of an "invincible ignorance." Though as late as 1863 Pope Pius IX could proclaim, "It is a well-known Catholic dogma that no one can be saved outside the Catholic Church" (DS 2867). He also argued that some people who remained outside because of "invincible ignorance" might be saved if they cooperated with divine grace.[1]

In *Lumen gentium*, Vatican II moved definitively beyond the traditional teaching. The Council fathers taught,

> Those also can attain to salvation who through no fault of their own do not know the Gospel of Christ or His Church, yet sincerely seek God and moved by grace strive by their deeds to do His will as it is known to them through the dictates of conscience. Nor does Divine Providence deny the helps necessary for salvation to those who, without blame on their part, have not yet arrived at an explicit knowledge of God and with His grace strive to live a good life. (*LG* 16)

In other words, God's saving grace is not confined to Christians. But the Council also taught that many, deceived by the Evil One, choose to serve the creature rather than the Creator.

Most Protestant missionary efforts began in the eighteenth century and continued under the influence of evangelical Christianity. Shaped by an austere Augustinian teaching on the total depravity of human nature after the Fall, they held that, with the loss of original righteousness, human beings, no longer free, were enslaved to sin. Even today, most evangelicals hold that salvation is possible only through a personal relationship with Jesus.

Unfortunately, with the missionaries also came European colonialism, often at the expense of the indigenous populations whose people died of disease, were enslaved, or sometimes were exterminated. What followed was "a system of plunder that viewed the geological and biological goods of the earth as resources that could be extracted without concern for local communities or ecologies."[2] In the Americas especially, millions died and much of their cultures was lost. The enslavement of others was an obvious evil, and the churches were slow and not always effective in confronting it. Some popes tried to forbid the slave trade or the enslavement of native peoples, but with little success; others allowed it. In the United States, bishops and some religious communities, including the Jesuits, "owned" enslaved people. Many Catholics supported the Confederacy in the Civil War.

The Church today is still divided, deeply polarized over questions of liturgy, social justice, economic and political life, and how to confront the racism that remains in our culture. Too often, there is an ignorance of history, both national and ecclesial, while the scandal of the sexual abuse of the young still lingers, though new safeguards and protocols are in place, not just in the United States but globally. The Church has lost many of its "professionals," its priests and religious, and some younger clerics do not welcome working collegially with the lay ministers, especially women, that followed Vatican II with the "explosion" of new lay ministries.

Today, many young adults are leaving the Church. A 2021 study by the Springtide Research Institute, an independent research organization affiliated with the Christian Brothers, said that 44 percent of Catholics aged between thirteen and twenty-five say that they do not belong to a church community. Those involved with the Church care strongly about gun control, 67 percent, and are closest to sharing concerns with other Catholics on this issue. But they reported the highest disparity between their values and what they believe their Church values on LGBT rights and income inequality, with two-thirds caring about LGBT issues.[3] Many consider the Church as too judgmental, concerned only about rules and doctrines, and out of touch with their lives and concerns. They also see the Church treating women as second-class members.

Pope Francis has called Catholics to be missionary disciples, but many are not sure how to carry out the Church's evangelical mission. Too many think that evangelization is for missionaries who go to other countries or Protestant evangelicals. And many, especially the young, are unfamiliar with the basic truths and doctrines of their faith. As James Heft says bluntly in a book on the future of Catholic higher education, most Catholic undergraduate students are religiously illiterate.[4]

Perhaps the greatest obstacle to belief today is the problem of suffering and evil. Next to it, arguments against the existence of God or the goodness of the Church pale into insignificance.

How many people today suffer from crushing poverty, a lack of justice, even violence? Think of the millions of victims of twentieth-century genocides: 1.5 million Armenians under the Ottoman government between 1914 and 1923; some three to seven million Ukrainians starved to death due to policies of the Soviet government, called the Holodomor, between 1932 and 1933; six million Jews in the Holocaust or Shoah and millions of others during the

Second World War; 1.7 million or more Cambodians killed by the Khmer Rouge between 1975 and 1979; and between 500,000 and a million Tutsi and moderate Hutus killed during the Rwandan genocide in 1994. All of these were innocent victims. To these should be added the hundreds of thousands who died from the atomic bombs dropped on Hiroshima and Nagasaki, as well as from the firebombing of German and Japanese cities during World War II.

Such tragedies are not just in the past. Consider the millions of men, women, and children maimed by the land mines sown in their farms and fields, the cynical use of political power for personal enrichment in so many countries, the young people growing up without hope, including the millions of refugee children stuck in camps, their futures circumscribed without adequate education. Statistics are impersonal. But they are staggering. And there are more victims recently in Ukraine, the result of Putin's brutal invasion.

Personal stories, heard or read, can break our hearts and move us to tears. A parent who has lost a beloved child in a mindless school shooting. A young adult whose promising life is cut short by a terrible accident. A young woman promised an *au pair* job in a foreign country, given transport across Europe, and then forced into prostitution to pay for airfare, room, and board. Migrants who pay coyotes much of their life savings, then are robbed, abandoned, or held for ransom when they call numbers given them for "the next step." Modern-day slavery, often unrecognized, traps an estimated forty million men, women, and children, victims of forced labor, child marriages, or bondage into debt. Three-quarters of them are women and girls, many of them victims of sexual trafficking.

In India, children under fourteen are forced to work for nine hours a day in brick kilns, breathing dust and chemically laden air, because their migrant or jobless parents have accumulated debts for housing that can never be paid off. In Uganda and Nigeria, children are kidnapped from their homes or schools: the boys are forced to commit acts of violence and murder against family members and peers to prevent them from returning home, while the girls are used as sex slaves. In some developed countries suicide is a growing problem. And we find similar examples in our own country.

Many wonder why an all-good God allows so much suffering, violence, and injustice. Is God angry with us? Why does God's presence seem so difficult to find, so obscure? I can't always share the enthusiasm of my Pentecostal friends. I want to experience myself a deeper relationship with the living God and to help others come to know Jesus, his Son, but the words often do not come. Like the Psalmist, I cry out, "How long, O LORD? Will you forget me forever? How long will you hide your face from me?" (Ps 13:1).

We need a new language, one that deals with experience and is invitational. Christianity cannot be imposed. A cultural Christianity is not authentic faith. Nor can we simply expect parents today to hand on the faith to their children. They are rarely equipped to do so. An inherited faith rarely bears fruit today. People need to discover the good news for themselves. How are we to help them do so?

Pope Francis wants a Church of missionary disciples; he says that a missionary style cannot be obsessed with the disjointed transmission of a multitude of doctrines to be insistently imposed (*EG* 35). As Massimo Borghesi has illustrated well, Francis takes for his model Pope Paul VI's 1975 apostolic exhortation *Evangelii nuntiandi*, calling it "the greatest pastoral document that has ever been written to this day," "the *magna carta* of evangelization." Like Francis himself, *Evangelii nuntiandi* avoids any reductionism of the Church's mission to either Christ or the Church, the gospel or human development, personal conversion or the reform of structures, holding evangelization and human development in a "balanced synthesis."[5]

Pope Benedict XVI says in his encyclical *Deus caritas est*, "Being Christian is not the result of an ethical choice or a lofty idea, but the encounter with an event, a person, which gives life a new horizon and a decisive direction" (no. 1). Francis makes the same point. At an international conference on his apostolic exhortation *Evangelii gaudium*, he said, "I would like to tell you very simply: the joy of the Gospel comes from the encounter with Jesus."[6]

So how do we preach the gospel today when so many no longer accept the old narratives? They no longer walk with us; so many have joined the "nones." How do we tell the Christian story? We can't simply fall into a biblical literalism, which makes little sense in a postmodern world. Nor can we reduce our faith to doctrines or ethical principles, though both are important. The Church continues its missionary work to bring the good news to those who have yet to hear it. But evangelization is not easy, especially for Catholics. It should be distinguished from proselytism, and yet the good news is meant to be proclaimed. How do we find the language today to convey that message?

The questions I have raised here are only some we hope to consider in this book. What follows are short chapters, brief meditations on these difficult questions, some of which I call "holy blasphemies," questions we are reluctant to raise with other Christians, though we often find ourselves asking them in the silence of our hearts.

ABBREVIATIONS

DOCUMENTS OF VATICAN II

DV   *Dei verbum*: Dogmatic Constitution on Divine Revelation

GS   *Gaudium et spes*: Pastoral Constitution on the Church in the Modern World

LG   *Lumen gentium*: Dogmatic Constitution on the Church

NA   *Nostra aetate*: Declaration on the Relationship of the Church to Non-Christian Religions

SC   *Sacrosanctum concilium*: Constitution on the Sacred Liturgy

UR   *Unitatis redintegratio*: Decree on Ecumenism

POPE FRANCIS

AL   *Amoris laetitia*: The Joy of Love

EG   *Evangelii gaudium*: The Joy of the Gospel

FT   *Fratelli tutti*: All Brothers: On Fraternity and Social Friendship

LS   *Laudato si'*: On Care for our Common Home

OTHER SOURCES

NABRE   New American Bible Revised Edition
WCC   World Council of Churches
DS   Denzinger-Schönmetzer, Compendium of Creeds,
         Definitions and Declarations on Matters of Faith and
         Morals

PART I

GOD
AND
CREATION

1

MORE THAN CHEMICAL INTERACTIONS?

I T ALL BEGAN WITH an initial explosion of high-density superheated mass, forming subatomic particles, then atoms and molecules, gases transformed into stars, planets, and ultimately galaxies. Each galaxy is a system of stars and star fragments, interstellar dust, gas, and dark matter, held together by gravity. The enormity of the cosmos is beyond comprehension. Separated by vast distances, the galaxies continue to expand, and thus the universe itself, as the galaxies continue to move away from each other.

We sometimes begin to sense the immensity of the universe on those rare nights when we can see the heavens above us, filled with stars. Seemingly near each other, the average distance between them is estimated by scientists at twenty million, million miles, while what is thought to be the actual number of stars is simply staggering. Only about six thousand stars are visible from earth, some of which burned out millions of years ago and whose light has only recently reached us. Our own galaxy, the Milky Way, consists of 100 to 400 billion stars and at least as many planets. It is only one of some two trillion galaxies in our observable universe.[1]

GOD AND CREATION

One of these planets—we call it Mother Earth—has, thanks to our astronauts, now become visible to us, a beautiful blue and white globe against the darkness of space, God's vast universe. On it, atoms, elements, and molecules continued to associate and combine over an estimated 4.5 billion years ago, developing into cellular life, microorganisms or microbes, and more complex multicellular organisms, bacteria, amino acids, plants, and, in time, animals, leading to the nearly one trillion species presently inhabiting our planet, including our own. Evolutionary theories chart and track this development.

The biblical story of creation is different; its focus is not on scientific description but ultimate causes. It begins in the Book of Genesis with two different accounts of God's great creative work. While mythical in form, their theological import is profound. The first is from the Priestly account; the second, from the Yahwist. The Priestly account is a reworking of the ancient Mesopotamian creation myth, the *Enuma elish* epic; it predates the Genesis story by at least a thousand years. A bloody cosmogony, it describes the conflict between Marduk, the chief god of the Babylonian pantheon, and Tiamat, a monster goddess associated with primordial chaos and the sea, later represented by a serpent or dragon.

Marduk overcomes Tiamat by filling her with air, then shooting an arrow into her heart, killing her. Slicing her in two, he places part of her above to form the dome of the sky or firmament and part below to form the earth. He then fashions the heavenly bodies, the sun and the moon, which themselves are divine, to be worshiped, and human beings to serve the gods. The figure of the chaos monster surfaces frequently in the Old Testament; it appears as the serpent Leviathan (Ps 74:13–15; Isa 27:1) or Rahab (Job 26:12–13), though now overcome by Israel's God, ultimately reduced to a creature playing in the sea (Ps 104:26).

How different from the Mesopotamian epic is the first creation account in Genesis! Here, God creates not by violence but effortlessly, by the sovereign power of the divine word. God speaks, and it is done. And it is good! As God's wind or spirit sweeps over the primeval waters, the "formless wasteland," God brings light out of darkness and separates the waters, making the dome above and gathering the waters below for the earth to appear. Then God brings forth fruit trees and plants of every kind. God creates the heavenly bodies, not to be worshiped, but to tell time, a subtle demythologization of the pagan myth. God then populates his creation, filling the waters with fish and the skies with birds, living creatures of all kinds, cattle, creeping things, the wild animals, and, finally, our own kind. There is a liturgical quality to this first story, with its repetition and response, "God saw how good it was," suggesting its use in the Temple worship. From the primordial chaos, God brings forth cosmos, a universe beautiful in its order and design.

In this first account, "man" (the word *'adam* in Hebrew means "humankind") is created in two kinds, male and female. "God created humankind in his image, in the image of God he created them; male and female he created them" (Gen 1:27). In other words, men and women are created together, in equality and mutuality. The second account has a different theme. God's fashioning the woman from Adam's rib suggests that they are made for each other, that the man is incomplete without her. Too often this has been forgotten in Christian theology, giving way to a view of male precedence rather than gender equality. The story of the Fall in Genesis 3 attributes male priority—"and he shall rule over you"—not to the order of creation but to sin.

Western theology has long placed a heavy emphasis on sin and, hence, on our need for redemption. In such a view, redemption entails Jesus paying a price with his bloody death on the cross to satisfy an offense against God's justice, thus restoring us to friendship with the Almighty, broken by the sin of our first parents. This is especially true for much of evangelical theology today, with its doctrine of substitutionary atonement, what might be described as a reparational Christology. But salvation is so much more than a narrow theology of atonement, not some satisfaction made to God, more than getting saved and being destined for heaven.

In contrast, the theology of the Christian East tends to stress the transformative character of the incarnation and accompanying divinization (*theosis*) of the human. The new *Directory for Catechesis* acknowledges the different approaches of the East and the West. Asking Anselm's old question, *Cur Deus Homo?* (Why did God become human?), the West answers, "To save us." The East responds, "So that we may become God." The new *Directory for Catechesis* sees both answers as complementary:

> God became human, so that humanity could become truly human as he intended and created him to be; humanity, whose icon is the Son; the human being, who is saved from evil and death, in order to participate in the divine nature. Believers can already experience this salvation here and now, but it will find its fullness in the resurrection. (no. 30)

Too often God's creative work is focused only on the Father. But creation is the work of the triune God. As early as 1 Corinthians (ca. 56 CE), Paul writes, "One God, the Father, from whom are all things and for whom we exist, and one Lord, Jesus Christ, through whom are all things and through whom we exist" (1 Cor 8:6). And in the Letter to the Colossians, what is probably an early Christian hymn, echoing the creation wisdom theology of Proverbs 8:22–31 and Wisdom 7:22—8:1, we read, "He is the image of the invisible God, the firstborn of all creation; for in him all things in heaven and on earth were created, things visible and invisible, whether thrones or dominions or rulers or powers—all things have been created through him and for him. He himself is before all things, and in him all things hold together" (Col 1:15–17).

The same theme appears in the Prologue to the Gospel of John, who begins his Gospel with another early Christian hymn, proclaiming that creation is in and through the Word:

> In the beginning was the Word, and the Word was with God, and the Word was God. He was in the beginning with God. All things came into being through him, and without him not one thing came into being. What has come into being in him was life, and the life was the light of all people. (John 1:1–4)

These works played a role in the development of the Church's Christology, seeing the Word of God that took on flesh in the person of Jesus as involved in God's creative work. No doubt they were influenced by Old Testament wisdom theology, which sees Wisdom as having a role in creation, created before all things (see Sir 1:4; Prov 8:22–24), present at creation (see Wis 7:22; 9:9), God's craftsman and delight, playing in God's presence (see Prov 8:30).

Creation is also the work of the Spirit, appearing so often in the Old Testament to express the dynamic, life-giving power of God (see Gen 1:1–2; Ps 104:30; Job 33:4), even though the doctrine of the Trinity was not fully formulated until the fourth century. Thus, a Christian creation theology and spirituality should be properly trinitarian.

Nor can creation be reduced to something that happened in the past. God's creative work is ongoing, a *creatio continua*, with the Word sharing God's life with us in what theology calls grace, the Spirit's presence in us and in the ongoing evolutionary process, the source of life so visible and dynamic. If God were not sustaining ourselves and the cosmos in this very moment, all would cease to exist, since our very existence is contingent on God whose very nature is to be. As Aquinas says, "The being of God, since it is not received into anything, but is pure being, is not limited to any particular mode of perfection of being, but contains all being within itself."[2]

We experience the life-giving Spirit, opening us to the divine presence in creation and calling us to share in that life. When we have eyes to see, we recognize that life in the happiness on the face of a child, in the play of the porpoise dancing on its tail, or in the birds splashing happily in the fountain. God's Spirit is working in our hearts, drawing us to truth, to beauty, to goodness with a longing for understanding, love, and communion. The materialist cannot fully appreciate the mystery of life; they cannot see beyond mere chemical interactions, cellular combinations, or embedded patterns.

The *Spiritual Exercises* concludes with an exercise Saint Ignatius calls the *Contemplatio ad Amorem*, the contemplation for obtaining love, a wonderful meditation on how God's creative work goes on, blessing us in so many ways. First, we are invited to consider the gifts of creation, redemption, and the specific gifts each of us has received. Then we are to consider how God dwells in his gifts, giving them life, sensation, and understanding, making us temples of his presence. In the third point, Ignatius asks us to imagine God working in creation, "as one who labors...in the heavens, the elements, the plants, the fruits, the cattle," sustaining them in being, animating them, giving them sensation. Finally, we are called to consider how all gifts and blessings descend from above, as justice, goodness, and mercy descend from God as rays of light from the sun or water from a fountain.

We can sense the divine energy in the dynamism of life, struggling to be and to flourish, overcoming obstacles, not always successfully. Paleontologists speak of species' death, the perishing of a whole class of creatures. A common figure for the number of species since life began on earth is thirty billion, but some put the number far higher. But of that total, whatever it might be, 99.99 percent of those species are no longer in existence.[3] And roughly 150 more disappear every day. Still, life goes on, endlessly reproducing itself in multiple forms. As Elizabeth Johnson describes it, "Neither overriding monarch nor absent deist god, the Spirit of God moves with extravagant divine generosity to create and sustain the conditions that have enabled the biodiverse community of life to become so interesting and beautiful."[4] As the Psalmist sings, "The heavens are telling the glory of God" (Ps 19:1).

What is more awesome than the stars spread out above us, glowing in the darkness of the night? And when we reflect on the vastness of the universe, the billions of stars and galaxies, the infinite dimensions of space, the energy that sustains the stars like our own sun—the star closest to us—how can we not sense a Creator? The drama of our expanding universe suggests that God's creative work has not come to an end; it is ongoing.

The Jesuit paleontologist Pierre Teilhard de Chardin presented a view of evolution that challenged the materialist view that life and mind could be reduced to chemical combinations, without any room for thought or spirit. At the heart of materiality, deep within the evolutionary process, Teilhard saw indeterminacy and relationality that one day would emerge in freedom and self-consciousness. And working in and through evolution he recognized the cosmic Christ, drawing us and all to unity. God is not finished with us.

2

THE SPARROW

OUTSIDE MY ROOM is a tiny patio. Every morning as I read the *Liturgy of the Hours*, I watch a small sparrow who comes to visit. I watch it hopping around the shrubbery or flying up to the higher branches in its search for the grains or insects that will be its breakfast. It seems a happy creature, small and vulnerable, but full of life, rejoicing just to be. And I often wonder: Does it enjoy its ability to jump up and fly? Of course, I know it is simply living out its sparrow nature in the biological patterns imprinted by ages of sparrow life. Still, like all life, its very existence is wonderful.

Watching it makes me more aware of the other small creatures that inhabit our campus. The always busy squirrels, running across the lawns or up the stucco walls of our buildings, watching us with quick-moving eyes. The cottontail rabbits that have recently reappeared, coming out at night to forage. The racoons, often with young ones in tow, climbing the trees. Or the hawks that bank and glide so gracefully on the breezes above our bluff.

It's not that I appreciate all nature. I've always feared snakes; they kill over 100,000 people each year. I hate mosquitoes, and the crows that come in large flocks, breaking the peace of the late afternoon with their loud, harsh caws, leaving our sidewalks filthy with signs of their passing. Or the great white sharks, now occasionally seen off our beaches, sometimes with deadly results. Great whites are amazingly designed eating machines, but I wouldn't want to run into one in the surf. Still, nature is wonderful, pulsing with life, in so many different and varied forms. The story of life is a great drama, a struggle to be and to flourish, not always successful, with many failures along the way, species that emerged and disappeared, leaving only fossilized remains buried deep in the earth. Thus, the story of life is not without loss or conflict.

For many of our animal cousins, life is a constant struggle for survival. To cope, nature has imprinted a predatory instinct within them and adapted their bodies for the kill. The Psalmist speaks of night when the beasts of the forest roam abroad and the young lions roar for their prey (see Ps 104:20–21). The poet Tennyson describes nature as "red in tooth and claw." Even the sparrow is a hunter. Our evolutionary inheritance has left its mark on us also. We too had once to struggle to survive, and many still do. We come not just from gatherers but hunters, like the young lions in Psalm 104. The predatory instinct still lurks within. Nor have we moved beyond war, as we so often learn to our sorrow. We still surpass any in the animal kingdom in our capacity for violence, an inclination that struggles against another toward communion.

Even the animal world exhibits a drive toward together-ness, for bonding or community. Many animals tend naturally to group. We speak of herds of cattle or elephants, flocks of sheep, packs of dogs, prides of lions, colonies of ants, schools of fish, and gaggles of geese. Animals often show signs of affection, emotions that will reach a fullness in humans. Mothers care with tenderness for their young, defending them fiercely or sometimes sacrificing themselves. Dogs greet their returning masters with unbounded excitement. They like to play, chasing after balls or catching fris-bees. Social media is full of cute little videos of dogs and cats who have become friends, playing together, or embracing each other. I have seen some videos of dogs or porpoises rescuing other small animals in danger.

Trees also have a social life. Recent studies see them exchanging carbon, water, nutrients, alarm signals, and hormones through their underground circuits, even with trees of different species. Resources flow from older trees to younger and smaller ones, while trees separated from their subterrain networks are more likely to wither and die.

The Creator shares the dynamism of life with creation, sustaining its growth in a *creatio continua*, calling it forward to a future yet unknown. From a Christian perspective, this drama is not accidental but purposeful, moving from the Word's role in creation—the Alpha and Omega, the beginning and the end—toward its ultimate fulfillment in God. Even if evolution exhibits characteristics of randomness and chance, it presupposes an underlying order in the physical and chemical structures of the material order. It is hard not to see God's creative spirit in this story of life, of relationship, of communion.

Materialists themselves cannot see this drama. One describes evolution as "a mindless, purposeless, algorithmic process."[1] For them, the natural world, even the human, is nothing but a mechanism, an evolutionary accident, the result of chance events leading only to more biological diversity and geological change.

Should we conclude that the incredible complexity of the universe is just an accident, or that the human body just "happened," a chance combination of atoms and molecules and microorganisms? Some scientists argue that there are as many atoms in just one molecule of our DNA as there are stars in most galaxies, and more atoms in a single human eye than all the stars in the known universe. But many scientists find no room in their scheme of things for freedom, or for an intelligence that reaches past what is experienced to ask about what might lie beyond. For them, the human person is a machine controlled by electrochemical processes. There is no spirit, no emergent self, no ethical center, but only embedded patterns and biochemical laws that control human behavior. Organisms and emotions are determined by algorithms. Meaning is created, not discovered. What cannot be known empirically cannot be real.[2]

Yet life, for all its energy, is finite, limited; the psalmist says that humans are like grass that dies; "in the morning it flourishes and is renewed; in the evening it fades and withers" (Ps 90:6). Faith tells us there is so much more. The God who created the heavens and the earth also sent his Son into the world, to offer us a share in the divine life. He spoke to us of the Father's love and called us his brothers and sisters, gathering a group of disciples to join him in proclaiming good news to the poor, liberty to captives, recovery of sight to the blind, and freedom for the oppressed. But his movement and claim to authority turned various religious and political leaders against him. Like so many victims of injustice and violence, he suffered a humiliating death on an instrument reserved by the Roman Empire for enemies of the state and escaped slaves. But death for Jesus was not the end. God raised him up to eternal life. His triumph over sin and death is our hope.

It is not so difficult for me to believe in God. God's mysterious presence seems so obvious in the beauty of the earth, the life that pulses in the sparrow, the complex physical, chemical, and biological relationships that support all life, or the spiritual creativity in our own kind that can produce *The Brothers Karamazov* or Beethoven's Fifth Symphony.

Believing that God took on human existence like my own in the person of Jesus is more difficult. I sometimes find myself in quiet moments asking uncomfortable questions that I would rather ignore. Can it really be true? Is this just another myth? And what is eternal life?

And yet the story of Jesus and his fate has left traces that suggest a historical foundation. First, there is the testimony of the early Christians in the New Testament documents, the Gospels and epistles. All of them focus on a Jesus not who was but who is still present in the Spirit. An extrabiblical testimony can be found in the work of Flavius Josephus, the Romano-Jewish historian; in his *Antiquity of the Jews* (93–94), he refers to Jesus and his death under Pilate, once several Christian interpolations are removed:

> Now there was about this time Jesus, a wise man. For he was a doer of startling deeds, a teacher of such men as receive the truth with pleasure. And he gained a following both among many Jews and many of Greek origin. And when Pilate, at the suggestion of the principal men amongst us, condemned him to the cross, those that loved him at the first did not forsake him. And the tribe of Christians, so named from him, are not extinct at this day.[3]

Josephus also refers to Herod Antipas ordering the death of John the Baptist as well as to James, the brother of Jesus. Finally, there is the remarkable growth of Christianity itself, which from a few followers of Jesus in Judea had expanded into much of the Roman Empire by the end of the first century.

Another important consideration for me, personally, is the nature of the human and its place in creation. Without falling into what Pope Francis calls in his encyclical *Laudato si'* a distorted or tyrannical anthropocentrism, the human person shows the highest development of consciousness or intelligence, indeed a reflective self-awareness. Humans not only know, but know that they know, and their consciousness constantly reaches beyond or transcends itself. We experience transcendence, even if we do not always recognize it for what it is. Our spirits are restless; they are not satisfied with present achievements or with a sense that what we see is all there is. Our questioning intelligence reaches beyond the immediate to the beyond: Why is there anything? Is there a benevolent presence yet to be revealed? Who am I really? When will my days come to an end? Animals do not ask these questions; I've yet to see a dog worried about climate change or what comes after death, but these concerns continue to challenge us. We are not content like the sparrow with the day's discoveries. We yearn for more; we seek to know and be known, to understand and be understood, to love and be loved.

It is in our capacity to love and be loved, and thus in community, that we become most fully human. Without others—relationships, society, communion—we are unable to realize our essentially social, trinitarian nature. Children cut off from normal human contact are incredibly damaged; their minds fail to develop; they are unable to learn language or develop a self-conscious awareness. We are made for one another, created to be in relationship, and find our fulfillment in community.

And if the interpersonal is the perfection of the human, how much more so is the divine. The union of mind and heart sometimes realized in human love finds its fullest expression in the perichoretic relations within the Trinity. God is profoundly personal. The three persons in God are not to be understood as individuals in our modern sense but in terms of their relations of origin. The Father who is unbegotten eternally begets the Son, the Spirit proceeds from the love and union between the Father and the Son. As Michael Downey has expressed these inner trinitarian relations, God is at once the Giver, the Given, and the Gift/ing. The Father is the Source of all Love; Christ, Son and Word, is Love Given; and the Spirit is the gift of Love, which is not static, but active and present.[4]

Thus, the language of persons expresses the essentially relational character of God's own life. In the divine, the notion of person fully realizes what it only suggests for us, that is, transcendence, openness to another, shared life, union, and, in a word, love. While the doctrine of the Trinity remains mystery, it suggests that relationality is at the very heart of the divine.

This is also the view of Pope Francis. In his often-poetic encyclical *Laudato si'*, he writes that, because of the "trinitarian dynamism" imprinted in each of us, "the human person grows more, matures more and is sanctified more to the extent that he or she enters into relationships, going out from themselves to live in communion with God, with others and with all creatures" (*LS* 240).

And Francis includes all creation in God's plan, making it holy in the Church's sacramental meal: "The Eucharist joins heaven and earth; it embraces and penetrates all creation. The world which came forth from God's hands returns to him in blessed and undivided adoration: in the bread of the Eucharist, 'creation is projected towards divinization, towards the holy wedding feast, towards unification with the Creator himself'" (*LS* 236). Our beautiful earth is in some way to be included in God's plan of salvation. Even my morning visitor, the happy little sparrow.

3

AN ANGRY GOD?

T HE GOD I LEARNED about as a child growing up in the
pre–Vatican II Church was a rather stern figure, an all-seeing
judge quick to punish or condemn those who strayed from the path
of righteousness. Though not unduly pious, I lived in fear of sins
committed or unconfessed. Indeed, those of my generation lived in
a culture of sin. Sin was everywhere. We were schooled with a clear
distinction between mortal and venial sin, the former involving
"grave matter." For those of us who were altar servers, touching
the sacred vessels with unconsecrated hands was a venial sin. The
rubrics for the priest specified that he committed venial sins by not
keeping thumb and forefinger together after the consecration, or by
not keeping the proper distance between his hands while praying.

As the name suggests, a mortal sin was deadly, cutting one
off from God and condemning him or her to eternal punishment
if left unconfessed. One hamburger deliberately eaten on Friday,
one intentionally missed Mass could send one to hell for all eternity. Sins of impurity were especially serious offenses, no "parvity
of matter," according to the moral theology manuals. All sexual sins
were serious. I remember a high school retreat directed by a Jesuit
notorious for his fixation on sins involving sex, with tragic stories

of those condemned to hell for one mortal sin. For many Catholic families, weekly confession was the norm, with long lines outside confessionals on Saturday afternoons. In Catholic grammar schools, students would be marched to church for confession before the monthly First Friday Mass.

How did the Church become so preoccupied with sin? Part of it can be traced to Saint Augustine, with his emphasis on the damage done to human nature by the sin of our first parents. Against Pelagius's stress on what human freedom alone could accomplish, apart from grace, Augustine taught that God does not command the impossible, imparting a rigorist dimension to Catholic moral teaching, which has endured. This is the same Augustine who, after finally ordering his own sexual life—"Give me chastity," he prayed, "but not yet"—taught that the only moral end of sexual intercourse was procreation. Even seeking pleasure in marital intercourse was at least venially sinful. The introduction of auricular confession in the sixth century and the development of Penitentials—manuals listing sins and the penances appropriate to each intended as an aid to confessors—contributed to the preoccupation with sin. It also tended to focus moral theology on confessors, rather than integrating it with a broader theology of life in Christ and the Spirit.

Augustine's theology, especially when read through the lens of John Calvin, also led to a heavy emphasis on sin. It impacted Catholic theology in the development of Jansenism in the seventeenth and eighteenth centuries. Originally the work of the Dutch theologian Cornelius Jansen (d. 1638), Jansenism became popular especially in France and centered in the convent at Port Royal-des-Champs. A radical form of Augustinianism, it stressed the debilitating effects of original sin, human depravity, the necessity of divine grace, and predestination. It also discouraged frequent reception of the Eucharist because of an assumed personal unworthiness.

With many Irish priests studying in France, Jansenism spread to Ireland and subsequently influenced Catholic culture in the United States. Some see Jansenism as a species of Catholic Calvinism. Calvin's radical Augustinianism also shaped much of American Protestantism, turning it into a narrow religion of "getting saved." A classic example was Jonathan Edwards's 1741 sermon, "Sinners in the Hands of an Angry God." Only a literalist reading of the Old Testament could lead to such a view of God.

I began to learn about a more gracious God at the same high school where the retreat master mentioned earlier had put the fear of God in us about sex. Shortly after that retreat, one Jesuit asked with a doubting look, "How long do you think its impact will last?" suggesting that perhaps the retreat didn't represent the last word. The Jesuits were good confessors, able to sooth an anxious heart. After entering the Jesuits myself, I encountered a gracious God and a merciful and compassionate Jesus in the Long Retreat, made by all Jesuits at the beginning of their formation.

And Vatican II did much to recenter the Catholic religious imagination, moving it away from a fortress-church mentality, defending Christians from the evil world, we had grown up with to an understanding of the Church as a sacrament of Christ in the world. It presented a picture of God who desires to share his divine life with us, adopting us as his sons and daughters, a God who even shares something of his truth and holiness in the teaching of other religions in his desire to bring all human beings into unity. The Council's Pastoral Constitution on the Church in the Modern World stressed the Church's concern for the poor, speaking of Christ crying out in the poor to beg the charity of his disciples (*GS* 88).

The postconciliar popes continued to stress God's love and mercy. Pope John Paul II described mercy as forming the image of his papacy, authoring the second of fourteen encyclicals, *Dives in misericordia*, Rich in Mercy, on the subject and establishing Divine Mercy Sunday on the Second Sunday of Easter as a feast for the entire Church. Pope Benedict XVI's first encyclical, *Deus caritas est* (2005), portrays love as the very nature of God, a passionate love for all humanity that "may certainly be called *eros*, yet it is also totally *agape*" (no. 9). He says that God's forgiving love is turned against his justice, reconciling the two (no. 10). In his remarks on Divine Mercy Sunday in 2008, he said that mercy "is the very name of God, the Face with which he revealed himself in the Old Covenant and fully in Jesus Christ."

Pope Francis has continued to stress the tenderness and mercy of God. Shortly after his election to the Chair of Peter, he described his now famous vision of the Church as a field hospital.[1] That November, he published his apostolic exhortation, *Evangelii gaudium*, The Joy of the Gospel, often seen as setting forth the priorities for his pontificate. He writes of a God who never tires of forgiving us, a God of tenderness and a mercy that is infinite. In 2015, he declared an "Extraordinary Jubilee of Mercy" (December 8, 2015, to November 20, 2016), even authorizing Archbishop Lefebvre's schismatic Society of Saint Pius X to confer validly sacramental absolution so that God's mercy might be even more available. A year later, he published a book titled *The Name of God Is Mercy*. In the introduction, he states beautifully, "God forgives not with a decree but with a caress."[2]

He brought the Jubilee Year to a close with an apostolic letter, *Misericordia et misera*, Mercy with Misery, a phrase of Augustine describing Jesus's encounter with the woman taken in adultery (see John 8:1–11). The letter speaks repeatedly of God's mercy, calling on Christians to create a culture of mercy, "a culture in which no one looks at another with indifference or turns away from the suffering of our brothers and sisters" (no. 20). His 2020 encyclical, *Fratelli tutti*, begins with the example of Saint Francis of Assisi, who, recognizing that God is love, gives us an example of how we too should show love for all people, stressing that we belong to a single human family.

In a beautiful book, written after his sister suffered a terrible accident that left her a quadriplegic, Fr. Richard Leonard tells us that in the months following, he received some of "the most appalling and frightening letters," like the one that said, "Tracey must have done something to deeply offend God, so that she had to be punished here on earth, for God will not be mocked!"[3] Such biblical literalism presumes an all-powerful God, a divine monarch whose agency rules over creation or at least tolerates evil as in some way contributing to the divine plan. How else would it answer the frequently posed question: "Why did God permit the Holocaust?" Such thinking leads to a violent rejection of religion or the death of faith.

But God does not punish us. He does not send us tragedy or pain to teach us a lesson. As the poet Annie Dillard says, "God is no more blinding people with glaucoma, or testing them with diabetes, or purifying them with spinal pain, or choreographing the seeding of tumor cells through lymph, or fiddling with chromosomes, than he is jimmying floodwaters or pitching tornados at towns."[4] These are natural evils, the results of the imperfection of the material, unstable air currents, geological fault lines, or bodily infections. Even more, the many acts of injustice, violence, and war that continue to victimize so many cause others to doubt the existence of God. How could a good God permit so much suffering, so much injury? These are moral evils. The fault here is ours: it resides in our selfishness, our self-centeredness, our failure to recognize and respect our common humanity. But so often our tendency is to blame God.

A more adequate theodicy, reflecting the kenotic image of Christ who "emptied" himself, giving up equality with God to take on the form of a slave (see Phil 2:6–7), describes a God who creates by "letting-be, by making room, and by withdrawing himself."[5]

This does not mean a God without power or agency but one who chooses to act in a nondominative way, a God who renounces violence or coercion, all signs of the demonic. The creation of a world of freedom implies a voluntary self-limitation of the divine power, or as Pope John Paul II once said, "In a certain sense one could say that confronted with our human freedom God decided to make himself 'impotent.'"[6] Our world has its own causality, and God does not encroach upon it.

But that does not mean that God is absent from creation; God is present throughout, working in and through natural causes, sharing his divine life with us, and flooding our hearts with his grace. Elizabeth Johnson writes, "At every moment divine agency will be physically undetectable. It is not a quantifiable property like mass or energy, not an additional factor in the equations, not an element that can be discovered among the forces of the universe at all. But in and through the creativity of nature, the boundless love of the Creator Spirit is bringing the world to birth."[7]

The Lord God who created the heavens and the earth through the Word is working through the evolutionary process, animating it through the Spirit as life struggles to be and to flourish, not all of it successfully, and yet novelty continues to emerge, and evolution unfolds on its way to fulfillment in God. The Jesuit paleontologist Teilhard de Chardin, whose thought inspired much of this thinking, speaks poetically of "the slow work of God," working in and through the evolutionary process. This God is continually sustaining creation, calling materiality, life, and ourselves to fulfillment in union with himself.

This also is the view of Scripture. Saint Paul describes creation as groaning in labor pains, hoping to be set free from slavery to corruption and share in the glorious freedom of the children of God (see Rom 8:20–22). The author of the Book of Revelation looks forward to a new heaven and a new earth (see Rev 21:1; 2 Pet

3:10–13). Jesus is "the Alpha and the Omega, the first and the last, the beginning and the end" (Rev 22:13). Creation through the Word will reach its fulfillment in union with the Word. Saint Paul sketches this when he says, "When everything is subjected to him, then the Son himself will [also] be subjected to the one who subjected everything to him, so that God may be all in all" (1 Cor 15:28). Our destiny is union with the divine.

So, evil will not have the last word. God does not hurl down thunderbolts like Zeus of old, but evil has its own disastrous consequences on evildoers. Those who do evil do not get off free. Their wounds are deep and often visible, for evil is toxic, alienating them from others, poisoning their souls, and destroying their humanity. Unable to genuinely love others, they often end up hating themselves. The field hospital Church of Pope Francis seeks to heal them.

The idea of final accountability is inseparable from Sacred Scripture. Pope Benedict XVI, in his beautiful encyclical *Spe salvi*, quotes Dostoevsky in his novel *The Brothers Karamazov*: "Evildoers, in the end, do not sit at table at the eternal banquet beside their victims without distinction, as though nothing had happened" (*SS* 44).

Will such evildoers also be saved? This remains mystery. Some have continued to hope that all would be saved. While the Catholic Church does not teach universal salvation, it does insist that God's saving grace is offered to all (see *LG* 16). And if it believes in the reality of hell, it has never named any specific human person as actually being condemned to hell. But, at the same time, the Church has not condemned the symbolic approach to a fiery hell of Origen, Gregory of Nyssa, and others.

David Bentley Hart argues that many in the first five Christian centuries believed that all would be saved. Without denying the existence of hell or the idea that the wicked would in some way be held accountable for their sins, following Paul, they saw the punishing fires in 1 Corinthians 3 as purifying rather than unending torment.[8] Hart maintains that a God who creates a world in which eternal suffering is possible, even if the result of one's free choice, could not be the infinitely good God of Christianity.

In response to the question about universal salvation, however, we can never forget God's mercy and God's love for his own. This is our compassionate God.

4

A SUBTLE PRESENCE

W HY DOES GOD seem so distant and so difficult to find? Does God reach out, disclose his mysterious presence? God's presence is subtle, "a tiny whispering sound" (see 1 Kgs 19:12); we need to be attentive. God does not overwhelm us to compel our belief or force our choices. God always respects our freedom, allowing us to find our own way, to make mistakes, learn from them, and grow. Still, God is amazingly generous in responding to us.

The story of Jesus meeting Zacchaeus in the Gospel of Luke is one of my favorites. A tax collector, Zacchaeus was short of stature. When he hears that Jesus will be passing by, he climbs a nearby syca-more tree to see him. For this small gesture he is richly rewarded. Looking up and seeing him, Jesus says, "Zacchaeus, hurry and come down; for I must stay at your house today" (Luke 19:5). Jesus not only welcomes him but pays him a visit.

People sometimes ask me why the disciples do not recognize Jesus when he appears to them after the resurrection. Their initial reaction is always doubt, fear, or nonrecognition. Some think they are seeing a ghost. Mary of Magdala does not recognize the man she so loves; she mistakes him for the gardener. A careful reading of these appearance stories suggests that the disciples too, like us, must be led to faith. If we decode them, each has something to teach us. Luke tells us that the two disciples on the road to Emmaus recognized him in the breaking of the bread (see Luke 24:35), a story with eucharistic implications, as the Church has recognized Jesus's presence in the Eucharist ever since.

Thomas, called the Doubter, wants evidence; he wants to see Jesus's wounds. According to John, his glorified body still bears them. They are not just his wounds, but ours. "Surely he has borne our infirmities and carried our diseases" (Isa 53:4). Jesus remains in solidarity with us. Our sorrows are not strange to him, our wounds foreign. After inviting Thomas to probe his wounds, Jesus says, "Have you believed because you have seen me? Blessed are those who have not seen and yet have come to believe" (John 20:29). The message is not just for Thomas; it is for us also. We don't need empirical evidence, proof to believe.

In Matthew, Jesus appears to the eleven on the mountain in Galilee. According to one possible translation, when they saw him, they worshiped him, "but some doubted" (Matt 28:17). Then Jesus gives them authority to teach and baptize, promising to remain with them until the end of the age (see Matt 28:19–20). The apostles and their successors have authority. Jesus will not desert his Church.

Unfortunately, too many Catholics still lack a deep familiarity with Scripture. In the sixteenth century, Martin Luther, himself a biblical scholar, recognized this as a problem. Without easily accessible vernacular translations, the Bible was available only to priests and scholars who could read it in Latin or its original languages. One of Luther's great achievements was his German translation of the Bible, making the biblical text more widely available and, in the process, helping shape the modern German language. As Protestant theology developed, it did so on the principle of *sola Scriptura*, "Scripture alone."

The Catholic reaction over the next five hundred years was to act as though the Bible was a Protestant book. Catholics of my generation did not have Bibles when we were growing up. Instead, we had books of Bible stories, often beautifully illustrated, including the Garden of Eden, Noah and the ark, Moses leading the children of Israel through the sea, David and Goliath, and so on. Biblical texts were read at Mass, but in Latin. We didn't have our own Bibles, lest we fall into the "Protestant error" of private interpretation. I still remember being asked to purchase a Bible when I was a senior in high school by our Jesuit teacher; what we received was a little, square, blue book associated with the English College at Douay in France, popularly known as the Douay-Rheims Bible. Based on the Latin Vulgate and approved by the Church, it went through several revisions to bring its dense Latinate vocabulary closer to the more readable King James Version. It remained the standard Catholic Bible until more modern translations began to appear in the mid-twentieth century.

Once I had this little Bible in my hand, I was so fascinated that I read it from Genesis to Revelation; it took me several months. It was Vatican II's Dogmatic Constitution on Divine Revelation, *Dei verbum*, that restored the biblical witness to its central place in the Church's life. Revelation is an important way God reaches out to us, disclosing or unveiling something of the divine mystery, even if indirectly. *Dei verbum* decreed that Scripture, "the soul of sacred theology," should nourish preaching, catechetics, and all Christian instruction, especially the liturgical homily (*DV* 24).

The Bible reflects the faith experience and story of Israel, the people of the first covenant. The New Testament puts us in touch with the Jesus tradition and the faith of the early Church. But it is not a magic book; Catholics are not biblical fundamentalists, constructing a theology on a few select passages or affirming that the Bible is without error in all its affirmations, including those about creation, history, doctrine, or attributed authors. Before there were written Christian texts there were churches, proclaiming their faith in the risen Jesus, repeating his words and parables, using christological titles, addressing God and Jesus in prayers and hymns, celebrating baptism and the Eucharist. The Bible is the book of the Church.[1]

Scripture is God's word in the words of human authors, inspired by God's Spirit. According to *Dei verbum*, revelation begins with the prophetic word, while "the deepest truth about God and the salvation of man shines out for our sake in Christ, who is both the mediator and the fullness of all revelation" (no. 2). In other words, revelation is not a text, as Islam teaches, nor a collection of inerrant propositions, as many fundamentalists hold, but a person: Jesus. Revelation is personal rather than propositional; it is trinitarian in form and christological in realization.

At the same time, God's revelation is more than literary. Our Catholic imagination is sacramental. It sees grace disclosed in nature and symbol; in persons, places, events; in ritual, art, story, and song. Sacraments are moments marked by the interplay of words, gestures, and earthen elements like bread, wine, oil, and water—symbols of God's grace, giving depth to our vision. The seven sacraments of the Church are symbols welcoming one into the community of faith, or sealing with the Spirit, or nourishing us with the bread of life and the cup of salvation, or pardoning the sinner, or celebrating spousal love, or showing God's embrace of the sick, or appointing to official ministry. They help us to recognize God's action in our lives. They can be deeply moving or sometimes, if done carelessly, reduced to mere routine. But they always invite our personal engagement. They are not magic.

During the COVID-19 pandemic, many have rediscovered the tradition of "spiritual" communion. Hungering for the Eucharist, their longing has been expressed in a desire to receive, to encounter the eucharistic Lord. And that hunger is indeed fruitful. As Karl Rahner taught, the grace of the sacraments, even the grace of the Eucharist, can be present apart from the sacrament itself, given the proper intentionality.

Nature itself is a kind of sacrament. As the Psalmist proclaims, "The heavens are telling the glory of God" (Ps 19:1). Expressing the creative, divine Spirit, nature is vital, generative, moving forward, transcending earlier forms—cellular, organic, living, conscious, and ultimately reflective. We see it struggling to flourish, overcoming obstacles, reproducing itself, supporting its offspring with hardwired maternal concern. Plants begin to grow again after two weeks on fire-scorched hillsides; sprouts of pine force their way through mountain rock formations; animal bodies, including our own, have a marvelous ability to heal themselves when injured. We marvel at nature's fecundity, the mystery and beauty of the night sky, the great herds and flocks that cover the African grasslands, or the intricacy of the human eye. Life is fascinating in all its forms, in its abundance, its beauty, even its struggle to survive. It suggests design, spirit, a Creator. We encounter God there.

The extroversion of contemporary life does not encourage interiority or reflection, let alone prayer. Individualism makes us self-obsessed, with little sense of community or the common good. The internet deluges us with information overload. But it also contributes to an epistemological problem. Social media is addictive and often narcissistic. Many young people load Instagram with hundreds of images of themselves or perform endlessly on TikTok. Meta bombards us with images and personal opinions; algorithms monitor the images we choose and target us with similar posts that reinforce our views and prejudices. There is no vetting of judgments; everyone is an authority. Few take the time to read newspapers or magazine articles, reducing what they know to soundbites reflective of their own opinions.

Cyberattacks are a new form of warfare. Foreign agencies hack into government computers, implanting destructive malware, stealing data, or spreading disinformation and falsehoods on social media platforms. Unscrupulous politicians spend millions to mainstream their propaganda, some in the attempt to create a parallel reality. When President Trump tried to claim that the election he lost to President Biden was fraudulent, Twitter and Facebook added ambiguous qualifications, "This is disputed and might be misleading." Finally, they closed his accounts. Others endlessly repeated the lie, calling into question the integrity of our electoral system. Some agitators, thanks to the widespread availability of miniaturized recording systems, make and post videos to spread their conspiracy theories.

Repressive governments control media to eliminate anything that might challenge their policies. In China, when Dr. Li Wenliang warned that a new virus was a danger to public health, authorities forced a shutdown of any report on his research. He was threatened by the police, who accused him of peddling rumors. But they weren't rumors. Shortly afterward, Dr. Li died of COVID-19. Millions were to follow him. Some news networks are more like ideological platforms, either of the right or of the left. They moved some to dismiss the lethality of the COVID-19 virus or argue that masks are ineffective and the vaccines dangerous. When Putin launched an invasion of Ukraine, Russian news sources were heavily censored; the word *war* could not be used.

Who is one to believe? The internet is a great resource. But a reliance on social media does not lead to wisdom. We find God's truth in Sacred Scripture and its celebration in the life of the Church. We need to learn how to identify objective sources and to assess what we read objectively. Universities should teach their students to think critically, unmask ideologies, recognize rhetorical fallacies, and open new horizons.

Most of all, we need to cultivate a contemplative sensibility, what the Buddhists call mindfulness. We need to recognize a God who watches over creation, not with domination and power, but always respecting our freedom, constantly calling us to himself, strengthening us with his grace. But God's presence is subtle. God continues to show us something of his glory, just as he did for Moses (see Exod 33:18–33), but the vision is always indirect, mediated by the beauty of nature, biblical stories, or the love and compassion of others. God's own love is overflowing.

5

A MODERN PROPHET

THE PROPHET'S VOCATION was not an easy one. The prophets rebuked a people they loved for their infidelity and their violation of the covenant; they accused them of worshiping false gods, oppressing the poor, and trusting in foreign alliances rather than in God. They continued to warn Israel that their violations of the covenant made God deaf to their prayers, that even their worship was loathsome because they would not listen to the plea of "the orphan, the widow, or the alien in the land," those without power or influence. For these offenses God's judgment would fall upon them, and they would be consumed by the sword. Thus, prophets are seldom popular. They unsettle our certainties, point out our sins, call us to conversion. They frequently face criticism, even persecution.

Isaiah and Jeremiah saw the pagan empires of Assyria and Babylon as Yahweh's instruments through which he would bring judgment on his people. Amos foretold military defeat and exile for Israel. Hosea accused Israel of playing the harlot, forsaking her jealous lover. Isaiah warned that their land would be a waste, its cities burned. Jeremiah predicted the loss of kingship, Temple, ark, and priestly instruction, and his ministry cost him dearly.

Jeremiah writes very personally, regretting the day he was born, wishing that his mother's womb had become his grave. He complains that the word of the Lord that once delighted him forces him to constantly reproach the people he loves, as he cries out violence and outrage. His message brings him mockery and derision, with even his friends denouncing him, calling for his downfall. But he is unable to remain silent; the word has become a fire burning in his bones, and he cannot hold it in. He fears that he must end his days in shame (see Jer 20:7–18). Nor was Jeremiah alone in his harsh message. Consider Isaiah, who spoke out on worship without justice and compassion (see Isa 1:11–16); or Ezekiel on religious leaders who lack compassion for the weak and the injured (see Ezek 34:4); or Amos (see 2:2–8; 7:21–24; 8:4–6).

Yet the prophets, Jeremiah among them, were not without hope. They preached that God's faithfulness to his people would yet prevail, that he would triumph over the forces that oppressed them, that his saving power would be manifested in a future yet unknown. They assured the people that God's salvation would break forth in a new way. The images vary, but always there is hope. A remnant would remain. God would raise up a future son of David, an anointed one or messiah who would bring justice for the poor. God would renew his covenant with his people, taking away their stony hearts and giving them natural hearts (Ezekiel), or make a new covenant with them, writing the law upon their hearts (Jeremiah). God's judgment, the Day of the Lord, would dawn over Israel, over the nations that oppressed them, over creation itself. God would bring the old order to a close and raise the dead to life (Daniel). In Second Isaiah, the mysterious figure of the Servant of the Lord appears. The Servant would bring God's salvation, gathering the people, giving his life as an offering for sin. Always there was hope.

Except for Amos. Not belonging to a class of professional prophets, Amos was a simple shepherd in the eighth century BCE, taken by God from his flocks to prophesize to Israel. He rebuked the people, especially the wealthy for their injustice, lying upon beds of ivory, taking advantage of the poor, cheating in their business practices, trampling the weak into the dust of the earth. He called out the leaders in Jerusalem who boasted,

> We will make the ephah small and the shekel great,
>   and practice deceit with false balances,
> buying the poor for silver
>   and the needy for a pair of sandals,
> and selling the sweepings of the wheat. (Amos 8:5–6)

But Amos was more cynical than the other prophets; he seems to have despaired of God's salvation. Proclaiming the Day of the Lord in negative terms—as a day of darkness, not light—he foresaw it bringing God's judgment, the overthrow of the sanctuary, the fall of the royal dynasty, and captivity for the people. There are no signs of hope in his oracles, no promise of future salvation, save for the last few verses, an epilogue that many scholars consider added several centuries later, after the exile.

Pope Francis sounds very much like an Old Testament prophet. Like Jeremiah, he has experienced personal disappointment and rejection in his ministry. Like Amos, he could at times sound cynical. As a young Jesuit priest, Jorge Mario Bergoglio had held several important positions in his province, including master of novices, provincial, and rector of a college. His charismatic leadership attracted an increasing number of young men to the Society. But he also was a figure of considerable controversy in his province. Even many of his brother Jesuits found him too conservative. He insisted on more traditional hymns at liturgy, clerical collars for students, and textbooks in Latin.

Not all Jesuits rejoiced when he was elected to the papacy, fearing the worst. Many had found his style of governance authoritarian, given to making hasty decisions; they considered him an ultraconservative. Later acknowledging his shortcomings, Francis stressed that he had never been a "right-winger," adding that making him provincial at thirty-six years of age was "crazy."[1] Admitting his mistakes, he tells us that his way of exercising leadership could be harsh.

But not all the criticism was deserved. Much of the opposition came from those Jesuits, many of them trained in Europe, who were committed to the liberation theology then popular in much of Latin America. Bergoglio found it too European, ideological, not attuned to the Latin American reality with the prominence it gave to popular religion, to the imaginative piety and emphasis on affectivity traditional in Spain and Latin America. His concern was always for a *teología del pueblo* (a popular theology or theology of the people), learned from his teachers in Argentina, Rafael Tello, Lucia Gera, and Juan Carlos Scannone.[2]

Far from being an ultraconservative, Bergoglio has always had a heart for the poor. As rector of the Colegio Maximo de San José, he established a farm, both to give the largely upper middle-class scholastics a personal experience of the lives of the poor and to provide food for the college and for the hungry of the neighborhood. He also provided shelter and bogus identities for those fleeing the repressive military-dictatorship during the "Dirty War" (1976–1983), and later, as bishop, he spoke out from his pulpit on behalf of trafficked women, abused children, and those victimized by the drug trade, calling out those mafia lords who paid for their meals in the fine restaurants of Buenos Aires with money stained with blood. He frequently reached out to the poor living in the city's *villas miserias* and recruited young priests to minister to them.

In his book *Let Us Dream*, Francis reflects on his disappointments, calling them his three "personal Covids," using the pandemic as a metaphor. The first was his struggle with pneumonia as a young man, a life-changing disease that resulted in the removal of part of one lung. The second came when he was sent to Frankfurt, Germany, ostensibly to study the language but really to get him out of Argentina. He reports missing his homeland so much that he would watch the planes taking off at night, dreaming of his return. The third was his exile to Córdova, Argentina, between 1990 and 1992, with little to do beyond saying Mass and hearing confessions. This Jesuit who had held such important positions was put on the shelf. But he also learned from the experience.

> It gave me greater tolerance, understanding, the ability to forgive, and a fresh empathy for the powerless. And patience: a lot of patience, which is the gift of understanding that important things need time, that change is organic, that there are limits and we have to work within them while keeping our eyes on the horizon, as Jesus did. I learned the importance of seeing the big in little things, and attending to the little in big things. It was a period of growth in many ways, the kind of new growth that happens after a harsh pruning.[3]

Important things need time; change is organic. This is one of his principles: "Time is more important than space." Pope John Paul II called this the "law of gradualness," the idea that we grow in virtue and in our relationship with God not at once, but over time.

Francis's approach to evangelization has largely been shaped by his concern for the disadvantaged, those at the "existential peripheries." Evangelization must include the social dimension of the gospel. It is much more than a call to be born again or return to the Church. In his programmatic apostolic exhortation, *Evangelii gaudium*, he writes, "To evangelize is to make the kingdom of God present in our world" (no. 176). Like Amos, he denounces an economy of exclusion, with everything subject to the laws of competition and the survival of the fittest, an economy in which the powerful feed upon the powerless. Citing Saint John Chrysostom, to the effect that "not to share one's wealth with the poor is to steal from them and to take away their livelihood," he points to the globalization of indifference, the idolatry of money, and the dictatorship of an impersonal economy, describing it as a new version of the golden calf (nos. 55–57).

He has taken particular aim at neoliberal "trickle-down" economics, a system embracing free-market capitalism and economic libertarianism that sees the market as the highest value, demanding that it remain free and unregulated. It holds that the role of the state is to enforce contracts and protect property. Social safety nets are not important; they only discourage self-discipline by permitting people to avoid the consequences of their decisions. He rejects the neo-libertarian argument that a free market will encourage economic growth, bringing greater justice and inclusiveness to the world: "This opinion, which has never been confirmed by the facts, expresses a crude and naïve trust in the goodness of those wielding economic power and in the sacralized workings of the prevailing economic system" (*EG* 54). Those who profit are the powerful and the wealthy.

For example, in 1965, the CEOs of the 350 largest firms in the United States earned 20 times as much as an average worker, but by 2017, they were earning 312 times as much. Meanwhile, the excluded are still waiting. Francis critiques the "inordinate consumption" that so damages the social fabric, noting that some simply blame the poor and poorer countries for their problems, another example of the old habit of blaming the victim. His teaching on the economy has generated considerable opposition in the United States.[4]

Francis has also frequently targeted clericalism. He raised this while visiting with Jesuits on a visit to Mozambique, saying, "One dimension of clericalism is the exclusive moral fixation on the sixth commandment....We focus on sex and then we do not give weight to social injustice, slander, gossip and lies. The Church today needs a profound conversion in this area."[5] In a letter to Cardinal Marc Ouellet in 2016, Francis called clericalism "one of the greatest distortions that Latin America has to confront."[6] Others have made similar comments. In a recent article in *Religión Digital*, José María Castillo wrote that the greatest threat to the Church is not schism but "fundamentalist clericalists" who impose what is in their interest and convenience, "even when that leads to the religious and evangelical abandonment of hundreds of thousands of Catholics."[7]

Clericalism reduces the laity to second-class citizens in the Church's life, privileging the ordained. It often infantilizes them, assuming an attitude of "Father knows best." Besides being an abuse of authority, clericalism represents a theological failure to acknowledge that laymen and laywomen share in the Church's mission in virtue of their baptism (*LG* 33). Thus, the fundamental sacrament of ministry is not orders but baptism.

As Pope John Paul II wrote in *Pastores dabo vobis*, Christ gives the ordained "a particular gift so that they can help the People of God to exercise faithfully and fully the common priesthood which it has received" (no. 17). Yet for many conservative priests, clericalism takes on a metaphysical dimension, as they maintain that ordination brings about an "ontological change" between the priest and other Christians, a view that makes little sense theologically and abets a false elitism that sees the ordained ministry as superior.

Pope Francis has a different vision of the Church's future. He has frequently noted that we are going through an era of "epochal change," brought on by changes in science and technology (*EG* 52). He returned to this theme in his address to the Roman Curia in

December 2019, calling for curial reform if the Church is to carry out its mission. In plain language, he said,

> Christendom no longer exists!...We are no longer living in a Christian world, because faith—especially in Europe, but also in a large part of the West—is no longer an evident presupposition of social life; indeed, faith is often rejected, derided, marginalized and ridiculed.[8]

His long-awaited document on curial reform finally appeared on March 19, 2022, the apostolic constitution, *Praedicate evangelium*. Among other amendments, it established five-year term limits, renewable once, for curial officials, after which they must return to their dioceses, and opened leadership positions in most of the dicasteries or congregations to any qualified baptized laypersons, women included.

Francis wants to help fashion a welcoming Church, famously comparing it to a field hospital or, to change the metaphor, a Church that is poor and for the poor, going to the peripheries. His vision of a transformed Church is of a community of missionary disciples, a transformation that demands a pastoral conversion not just of the faithful but also of the papacy and the Church's central structures. He wants the Church to reach out to those of other religious traditions, particularly Muslims, to move beyond the culture wars, with their near-exclusive focus on abortion and same-sex marriage, and to address the plight of immigrants, the poor, and the environment.

From the beginning of his papacy, he has spoken out against the hundreds of thousands suffering from what he calls "an economy of exclusion and inequality," an economy that kills (*EG* 53). In his encyclical *Fratelli tutti* (2020), he spoke out against modern-day slavery, war, the death penalty, and racism. The plight of migrants has been a particular concern. Shortly after his election to the Chair of Peter, he visited Lampedusa, a tiny island in the Mediterranean between Tunisia and Italy overwhelmed by thousands of migrants arriving on damaged, unstable boats, while many others perished at sea. In a homily on what he called a "globalization of indifference," he noted, "We have become used to the suffering of others: it doesn't affect me; it doesn't concern me; it's none of my business!"[9] What should be our response? "Welcome, protect, promote, and integrate" (FT 129).

To address these issues, he calls for an intergenerational, interdisciplinary dialogue embracing a variety of perspectives and different fields of knowledge. How different this would be from the narrow perspectives of talk radio, conspiracy theories, and social media tailored to the views of its subscribers.

All of this has brought about considerable pushback from conservative Catholics, many of them wealthy business leaders as well as a considerable number of bishops. Most begin with issues such as marriage and the family, same-sex marriage, and Francis's opposition to the death penalty, but they quickly segue to a critique of his teaching on the economy, the environment, and immigration. One finds little support for these issues in conservative media, as well as for efforts for greater racial and financial equality.[10] Such issues are ignored by EWTN.

Nor did the USCCB speak out on these issues during the Trump years, but when Joseph Biden was elected president in 2020, only the second Catholic president in the history of the United States, and perhaps the most Catholic, some of the bishops sought to exclude him from holy communion because of his support for legal abortion, the then-established law of the land. Francis has often spoken against abortion, with particular emphasis in his encyclical Laudato si'. While the Church continues to oppose abortion, Rome's counsel was to work for unity.

Thus, Francis will be remembered as a modern-day prophet. For some, his preaching remains unpopular. His third encyclical is an eloquent plea for recognizing that we belong to one human family, that we need to work together for justice and peace. This is not so different from the message of the Old Testament prophets, but now expanded globally.

PART II

CHRIST
AND
HIS BODY

6

ADVENT REFLECTIONS

A S THE LITURGICAL YEAR draws to a close, the Church places before us various apocalyptic passages from the Gospels, stories of the last days, with the darkening of the heavenly bodies, the stars falling from heaven, earthquakes and roaring seas, nations rising against nations, false prophets leading many astray. These are frightening texts, based on Mark's conflating Jesus's prediction of the destruction of Jerusalem with the Son of Man's final coming in power and glory. But how that will all come about remains shrouded in mystery.

Physicists, building on the second law of thermodynamics, foresee a time billions of years in the future when, according to the principle of entropy, the universe runs out of energy. With everything reaching the same temperature, the result will be a heat death, rendering the material world disordered and inert. We could bring those final days so much closer ourselves, destroying this beautiful planet with a mindless exchange of nuclear bombs and missiles, the tragic result of the new arms race presently underway as we continue to modernize our nuclear weapons, develop the next generation of delivery systems, and confront new wars, most recently in Yemen, Ethiopia, and Ukraine.

Conservative evangelicals talk about the rapture, when Christ comes down from heaven to lift the righteous up from the dead—read, those who have been born again—out of this vale of tears to bring them into the eternal kingdom (see 1 Thess 4:16–17). Catholics, belonging to a false church, as some fundamentalists argue, will be left behind.[1] When I was a child and our mother used to read to us bedtime stories, one of my favorite characters was James Thurber's "Get Ready Man," apparently a historical individual who roams through his stories shouting, "Get Ready! Get Ready! The world is coming to an end."

My own sense is that Christ comes to us with far less drama. A wonderful hymn called "The Canticle of the Gift," sometimes heard at Christmas, proclaims, "In the stillness of the night when the world was asleep, the almighty Word leapt out. He came to Mary, he came to us. Christ came to the land of Galilee." The picture here is of God's silent coming, less dramatic than the gospel stories with choirs of singing angels, visiting shepherds, and wise men from the East. And perhaps truer to life.

Many would prefer something more impressive. Even in the time of Jesus, people wanted more. He rebuked the Galileans, "Unless you see signs and wonders you will not believe" (John 4:48). The scribes and Pharisees asked him to show them a sign (see Matt 12:38). Those standing around the cross demanded, "Let the Messiah, the King of Israel, come down from the cross now, so that we may see and believe" (Mark 15:32). In our own day, there are many whose faith seems to require signs and wonders; they are easily drawn to what seem to be manifestations of the miraculous or the supernatural, visions of Our Lady—some 2,500 claimed over the centuries—weeping statues, bleeding hosts, incorruptible bodies of the saints.

Millions visit shrines where Mary is said to have appeared, some six million to Fatima alone each year. The Church is reluctant to discourage these expressions of popular piety, but even those few apparitions approved by the Church remain in the category of private revelation; they are not essential to the Church's faith. With traces of the transcendent banished from our culture, it reappears in bogus form in so many films today, films full of superheroes, demonic figures, or time travel.

The Johannine Prologue, a pre-Johannine Christian hymn, tells us that the Word, through whom the heavens and the earth were made, the true light, was coming into the world, the world that came to be through him, and yet the world did not know him (see John 1:10). For God comes to us quietly, without drama. He comes in the stillness of the night. The world goes on as before. But everything is different.

For God takes on flesh in our own graced but damaged humanity, in a world with so much poverty, so much hunger, with so much oppression and injustice, so much sin. We are familiar with our own sins and failings, the mistakes we've made, the things we regret, the damaged relationships, the issues with which we continue to struggle. Our families are imperfect, with unhealed wounds.

And our relationships are not just personal; they are also economic, racial, and ecological. Our world is full of suffering, so little hope for those on the margins of our Western prosperity, for those who struggle to survive at the peripheries. Our cultures are often scarred by prejudice against those who are different. The suffering of the innocent is perhaps the greatest obstacle to faith today. Our beautiful planet, our sister, Mother Earth is itself in jeopardy, as Pope Francis has written in his encyclical *Laudato si'*. Even our Church is sinful, as we have become so painfully aware. We long for God's salvation.

During the Advent season, we frequently hear the liturgical refrain "Let justice descend, you heavens, like dew from above.... Let the earth open and salvation bud forth" (Isa 45:8, NABRE). The early Christians had this sense that God's salvation was near.

They worshiped with their altars facing East, where Christ would return like the rising sun; they prayed *Maranatha*, Come, Lord (see 1 Cor 16:22; Didache 10:14; Rev 22:20), in anticipation of his saving presence. But by the Middle Ages, his coming morphed into dread of the Last Judgment, often represented on the tympana of so many cathedrals. His coming was feared, rather than anticipated.

Today, God seems silent. God does not speak; he does not appear to answer our prayers or reveal the divine presence. But is God truly absent?

Our faith tells us that God's salvation has indeed appeared but not in supernatural displays or dramatic interventions. As Elijah tells us, God is not in the wind crushing the rocks, nor in earthquakes, nor in fire, but in a tiny whispering sound (see 1 Kgs 19:11–12). God comes silently; we must watch and listen carefully. We learn to recognize his presence in reflective moments. We need to develop habits of silent attentiveness, contemplative habits, learning to trust what Teilhard de Chardin calls the slow work of God.[2] We need to put aside our habitual impatience, taking time to let our ideas develop and mature, to see where God might be leading us.

This is what the holy season of Advent is about. It is a time, four short weeks, when we slow down to ask and reflect on how God is coming into our lives. We discover him frequently in the events of our families, with their crises, challenges, painful moments when we are tested and in moments of joy when we give thanks. We often encounter him in a chance conversation with a stranger or a friend. When we help someone in need or accept forgiveness for a wrong done, God is there. We see God in the face of a child, full of beauty, or in those quiet moments when we contemplate the stars on a dark night and realize that this beautiful cosmos is not some accident, a mere assemblage of atoms and particles, a mechanism lacking purpose and Spirit. We've all had those moments when we sense so much more.

48

Theologians like Elizabeth Johnson, John Haught, and Ilia Delio tell us that God's Spirit is at work, unseen in the evolutionary process that shaped the heavens and the earth, drawing all things to Christ and to God, echoing Teilhard de Chardin who himself echoes Saint Paul's vision of a creation yearning to be set free from corruption, moving toward that day when God will be all in all (see Rom 8:21; 1 Cor 15:28).

But we need to remember that God works through us, reaching out through our acts of compassion and care to touch others. It's not enough to reduce the gospel to the "Great Commission" at the end of Matthew, where Jesus sends his disciples forth, telling them to "make disciples of all nations, baptizing them in the name of the Father and of the Son and of the Holy Spirit" (Matt 28:19). Though Catholics could certainly be more evangelical, more willing to share their faith with others, they find the heart of the gospel in the Beatitudes, in the Sermon on the Mount, and in the great eschatological sermon often called "the Judgment of the Nations" (Matt 25:31–46), where Jesus tells us that we find him in the hungry, the thirsty, the stranger or immigrant, those without clothes or in prison. Jesus does not appear in the Gospels as a moralistic teacher. We need to act compassionately, as God does.

Compassion can heal wounds and open hearts. And it can transform us, teaching us to be gentle, tender, and loving. We begin to experience love ourselves. Recognizing in the eyes of another that we ourselves are loved, we begin to experience the love of God. Like a lover, God wants to share his life with us. But we need to be attentive.

Advent is the season when we prepare for his coming; it is a time for watching and waiting. I love its symbols, the Advent wreath, with the sharp smell of its pine branches suggesting freshness, the earth, life. I love the gradual lighting of its candles, like God's coming into our world and into our lives. I love the hope expressed in the liturgical readings, especially those from the Old Testament prophets. I love the Advent hymn "O Come, O Come, Emmanuel."

Too often we rush this beautiful season. Radio stations begin playing Christmas carols two weeks before Thanksgiving. Christmas trees, lights, and Santa Claus figures break out in stores. But these symbols are not calling us to prayer. They say, "Buy, buy, buy!"

Advent is a holy season. It deserves a certain soberness. So watch, be ready, pray. God is near; the sacred is all around us, indeed within us.

7

THE KINGDOM AND SALVATION

WHEN I ASK MY STUDENTS what Jesus preached, if they say anything at all, it's usually a variant of the Golden Rule: do unto others as you would have them do unto you. (Once a student said, do unto others before they do it to you.) Thus, they reduce Jesus's message to one of universal love. While that certainly is one of the implications of his preaching, it's not entirely correct. What Jesus proclaimed in his sayings and parables and compassionate acts is the nearness of the kingdom or reign of God. The reign of God was his term for salvation, the image or metaphor that dominated his preaching.

Too often conservative American Christianity has reduced Jesus's message to an otherworldly or purely individualistic spiritual concept; salvation means "getting saved," "being born again," or accepting Jesus as one's personal Lord and Savior, putting one on the fast track for heaven. For some "hyper Calvinists," it even means salvation as something that once gained can't be lost, or, as they say, "once saved, always saved."

But this is far different from the biblical view of salvation, from what Jesus means by the reign of God. We need to unpack his metaphor. The biblical concept of salvation is far richer, deeper than "saving one's soul." It is not just a spiritual reality but something that touches our lives, our bodies, our spirits, even creation itself. For ancient Israel, God's salvation meant that God had chosen them to be a people peculiarly his own; he promised to accompany them, guide them, giving them his law, protecting them from their enemies, and leading them into the land of promise. For example, Isaiah says, "Be strong, do not fear! Here is your God....He will come and save you" (Isa 35:4). He speaks of a God who will open the eyes of the blind and the ears of the deaf, empower the lame to leap like a stag and the tongue of the mute to sing. Even more, streams of water will burst forth in the desert, making pools in the burning sands (see Isa 35:4–7).

Among the metaphors Israel used for its God—images like shepherd, rock, and savior—was the image of Yahweh as king. The royal psalms repeatedly celebrate God as a king who rules over Israel, over all the nations, over creation itself (see Pss 93, 95, 96, 98, 99). Today, many find this image too patriarchal, but for the ancients, a king had absolute power, literally the power of life and death over his subjects. So, it was natural to see royal power in the divine.

Certainly, this imagery was basic to Jesus's religious imagination, but scholars tell us that he may well have been the first to use the actual phrase "kingdom of God." In his preaching, the kingdom of God, or, more accurately, the reign of God, meant God's power, grace, and justice, in a word, God's salvation, breaking in to people's lives, their bodies, and the world in a new way. The kingdom or reign of God in his preaching was both present and still to come in its fullness, as a careful reading of Matthew 13 makes clear.

In his first sermon at Nazareth, Jesus echoes the prophet Isaiah in proclaiming,

> The Spirit of the Lord is upon me,
>> because he has anointed me
>>> to bring good news to the poor.
> He has sent me to proclaim release to the captives
>> and recovery of sight to the blind,
>>> to let the oppressed go free,
> to proclaim the year of the Lord's favor. (Luke 4:18–19)

Jesus called the poor, the hungry, the thirsty, the naked, the alien, and the imprisoned blessed (see Matt 5:3–12; Luke 6:20–26) and said we will be judged on how we respond to them (see Matt 25:31–46). Proclaiming the poor or the hungry blessed was a sign of God's special care for the disadvantaged or the needy. God's grace or power was embracing them.

Pope Paul VI echoed Jesus's words in his great apostolic exhortation *Evangelii nuntiandi*, when he wrote, "Christ proclaims salvation, this great gift of God which is liberation from everything that oppresses man but which is above all liberation from sin and the Evil One" (no. 9). Similarly, when Jesus cleansed a leper, freed someone from an evil spirit, healed a paralyzed man, or cured a woman from a hemorrhage of blood, it was not just a sign of God's healing grace but also a restoration of the person to the community from which they had been banished because of their disease.

The Epistle of James, dismissed as a "letter of straw" by Martin Luther for stressing that faith without works is dead, might be described as teaching the "ethics of the kingdom." The author of the epistle rebukes those who give special attention to the elegantly dressed while ignoring the poor who come into the assembly in shabby clothes (Jas 2). Perhaps the best expression comes from

Saint Paul: "The kingdom of God is not food and drink but righteousness and peace and joy in the Holy Spirit" (Rom 14:17).

The fathers of the Church continued this tradition. Ambrose said, feed the hungry, for if you do not feed him, then as far as you are concerned, you have killed him. According to Basil, "When a man strips another of his clothes, he is called a thief. Should not a man who has the power to clothe the naked but does not do so be called the same?" Augustine wrote that "the superfluities of the rich are the necessities of the poor," while John Chrysostom said that "not to enable the poor to share in our goods is to steal from them and deprive them of life, for the goods we possess are not ours, but theirs."

Pope Francis writes in the preface to a book on his social teaching: "Every one of us can contribute to realizing the work of the Reign of God on earth, opening up spaces of salvation and liberation, sowing hope, challenging the deadly logics of egoism with the brotherly and sisterly spirit of the Gospel, dedicating ourselves in tenderness and solidarity for the benefit of our neighbors, especially the poorest."[1]

Thus, witnessing to the kingdom of God means more than simply charity; it means also challenging the structures of injustice that disadvantage so many. If we simply accept the crushing poverty that cripples lives, if we tolerate injustice or reduce racism to personal relationships, overlooking the cultural structures of white supremacy and systematic racism that so disadvantage others, if we ignore the homeless or leave children to an inferior education in neighborhoods blighted by poverty and neglect, if we treat women as second-class citizens or refuse the ecological conversion that Pope Francis calls us to—we are not witnessing to the reign of God.

So too, the Church that carries on Jesus's mission must include the transformation or humanization of the world in the fullest sense; it includes the struggle for justice, peace, and human rights. Where violence, war, racism, injustice, the exploitation of the poor rule, the kingdom of God is not present. Too often, however, when a priest or deacon speaks this way in a homily, some immediately object that he is turning to politics, not the gospel.

Does the mission of the Church then have a political dimension? Of course! Not in the sense of partisan politics, which today are so poisonous, but precisely because our vocation and the Church's mission is lived out in the world. The word *politics* is derived from the Greek *polis*, meaning city. Thus, to be political is to be involved in civic life, in the life of the city. Witnessing to salvation is not just a personal matter; it always unites us with others. There is a social dimension of the gospel.

Our Christian faith is not something that exempts us from the life of the world but is precisely something to be lived out in the world. Edith Stein, the Jewish philosopher and convert to Catholicism who died at Auschwitz, now known as Saint Teresa Benedicta of the Cross, describes coming to the realization that "even in the contemplative life, one may not sever the connection with the world. I even believe that the deeper one is drawn into God, the more one must 'go out of oneself'; that is, one must go to the world in order to carry the divine life into it."[2] In a similar vein, Dom Helder Câmara, bishop of Recife in Brazil and declared a Servant of God in 2015, is quoted as saying, "When I feed the poor, they call me a saint; when I ask why they are poor, they call me a communist."

We live today in a world of global inequities, political oppression, and poverty. And the gap between the prosperous and the destitute continues to grow. The number of migrants and refugees for 2019 displaced from their homes by war, violence, climate change, and persecution reached an all-time high, almost 70.8 million, according to the United Nations High Commissioner for Refugees. The war in Ukraine added several million more. Thousands drown as overloaded vessels capsize or are victims of those who prey on them as they make their way over land. Many of the world's poor suffer from inadequate health care, even in our own country. Their health is damaged by inadequate diets, unhealthy living conditions in slums and ghettos, and improper sanitation. An economy of exclusion disadvantages millions of people.

Closer to home, we can think of the casual disregard for the poor and the powerless, the violence in our inner cities, the children caught up in the culture of gangs, drive-by shootings, lives wasted by drugs—crystal meth for the poor, designer cocaine for the well-to-do—or suffering physical or sexual abuse from relatives or other trusted adults, often even from priests. We think of the billions of dollars spent on weapons of war, the threat of terrorism, the pornography and abortion industries, and the thousands who are homeless, reduced to living on the streets.

And yet so many of those with power and means, including many who profess to be Christians, seem not to care. In the United States, many people refuse to acknowledge the systemic racism and white supremacy that so corrupts our culture. They support those who, in the name of a populist nationalism, refuse to welcome refugees or do not object to separating children from their parents, warehousing them in inadequate shelters, to discourage immigration. Many people support a runaway gun culture that admits of no limits and has led to the murder of children in their schools and worshipers at their religious services, and they refuse to acknowledge the reality of climate change and the ruination of the environment. They are against a government-subsidized health-care system, which could provide relief for the millions who cannot afford the high cost of medical care today.

Many refuse any limitations on access to abortion, which continues to deny the dignity of human life, as does the death penalty. These are examples of what Pope Francis calls a "throw-away" culture in which human beings can be simply discarded. The digital age brought into our homes by the internet provides us with more information than we can digest, while social media, rather than bringing us closer together, has highlighted divisions. We are increasingly polarized, with poisonous relations in society, government, and even the Church. Meanwhile, the gap between the very rich and the very poor continues to grow.

At the same time, the grace of salvation also reaches beyond this world. The resurrection of Jesus means not just that God raised Jesus from the dead but that we too will be raised up. We remind ourselves of this and pray for the deceased when we celebrate the Mass of Christian Burial. It is a deeply consoling liturgy. Now in my seniority, I read the obituaries each day in the paper and continue to marvel at so many in our secular age whose deaths are observed, not with prayers and the rituals of faith, but with a "celebration of life," often in a local restaurant. Or frequently one reads, "No services will be held."

Still, we find it difficult to imagine life in the world to come. What is the nature of the risen body? It remains a mystery. Andrew Greeley compares the risen life to the physical ecstasy and emotional satisfaction of intercourse between two people deeply in love. Its joys will be physical, sexual, interpersonal, and corporate.[3] Shocking though this may be, such imagery was often used by mystics such as Teresa of Avila and John of the Cross to describe the experience of mystical union, which after all is the deepest meaning of heaven. The prophet Isaiah also used sensual images to suggest God's salvation, a feast with rich food and fine wines (see Isa 25:6), or a kingdom of justice and peace where the wolf will be the guest of the lamb and the bear and the cow will be friends (see Isa 11:6–7). God's salvation will satisfy all of our hungers; it will be a kingdom of peace, justice, and love.

Even more, the resurrection of Jesus embraces not just our own destiny but also this beautiful planet, glowing blue and white in the darkness of space. Jesus is the "firstfruits" of the resurrection of the dead, and when death itself is destroyed, everything will be subjected to him, and "the Son himself will also be subjected to the one who put all things in subjection under him, so that God may be all in all" (1 Cor 15:28). What a wonderful vision! The Book of Revelation looks forward to the day when God will dwell with his people, wiping away every tear from their eyes, "death will be no more; mourning and crying and pain will be no more, for the first things have passed away" (Rev 21:3–4).

The vision of Scripture is that nothing should be lost, for creation itself shares in God's salvation (*EG* 4), prefigured in the resurrection of Jesus. In *Laudato si'*, Pope Francis sees this already happening at Mass: "The Eucharist joins heaven and earth; it embraces and penetrates all creation. The world which came forth from God's hands returns to him in blessed and undivided adoration: in the bread of the Eucharist, 'creation is projected towards divinization, towards the holy wedding feast, towards unification with the Creator himself'" (no. 236). God's saving work is not over; it has just begun.

8

THE PASSION

IF THE INJUSTICE AND SUFFERING of so many people is the strongest argument against the existence of God, it's important to note that God also shares in that injustice and suffering in the person of his beloved Son. But the story of the passion and death of Jesus is not easy for many of us to contemplate. We see Jesus deserted by his companions; arrested and abused by those who opposed, mocked, scourged, and judged him unfairly; and sent on that terrible journey to Calvary that ends with his crucifixion. For a meditation on the passion of the Lord, I would like to suggest four images.

The first comes from an ecumenical monastery of the Sisters of Grandchamp in Switzerland. Grandchamp is an ecumenical community on the shores of Lake Neuchâtel, near the city that bears its name. The sisters come from different churches and nations; their life is one of prayer, reconciliation, and hospitality, welcoming the many who come to pause for a while, to join in the prayer and refresh their own faith. It is a place of peace. Their chapel, on the second floor of a wooden barn that was once a shed for dyeing and drying garments, is warmly lit by colored lights—reds, blues, ambers, and greens—filtering through openings in the slats that comprise the walls. In the center is a low altar, surrounded by a few pews and the prayer stools that are common in Europe.

As you enter, set off in a separate room is a crucifix, lit by a single votive candle. The Christus on it is a tortured figure, naked and exposed. It is Jesus humiliated and alone, forsaken by his friends, apparently even by his God. Spurned and avoided by men, a man of suffering, accustomed to infirmity, we held him in no esteem, as Isaiah wrote prophetically (see Isa 53:3).

The cross is the work of Guido Rocha, a Brazilian artist who was himself tortured by military dictatorships in Brazil and later in Chile. Some find it a difficult image to behold, a tormented face, limbs elongated like a Giacometti statue. They protest that it is too grim, that it shows no hope, only pain. But it is Jesus in his agony. Jesus, who must have been tempted to despair seeing his mission apparently ending in failure and disgrace as he was mocked by the bystanders and those who put him on the cross. But he did not despair; he clung to the one he called "Abba," the One he sought always in prayer, early in the morning and at the end of each day, praying now, "Father, into your hands, I commend my spirit."

A second image is a painting I once saw of the crucified Jesus, his blood flowing down the wood of the cross and into the ground beneath, mingling with Mother Earth in all its physicality and materiality, the divine mixing with the earthly as in our own bodies, consecrating both, uniting us into one body, his Body in which he remains present to us and to the world.

We know how Jesus identifies with those in need, makes them his own, calling them his brothers and sisters. When Saul of Tarsus, soon to be known as Paul, was making murderous threats against the early followers of Jesus he heard Jesus ask in a vision, "Saul, Saul, why do you persecute me?" (Acts 9:4). In the great vision of the eschatological judgment in Matthew 25, Jesus says to those who did not recognize him in the stranger—whether hungry or thirsty or naked or in prison—and minister to them, "You that are accursed, depart from me" (Matt 25:41). If we have learned anything from the COVID-19 pandemic, it is how closely we are related to each other and how devasting any refusal to care for each other by taking proper precautions, such as wearing masks when appropriate and getting vaccinated, can be.

And the crucifixion is still going on, in all the innocent who suffer violence, in the humiliation and exclusion of those who are vulnerable or different, in the lives of immigrants on troubled waters, packed into unsafe boats by unscrupulous human smugglers or separated from their children by government agents. The crucifixion continues in those who are tortured or abused or discriminated against because of the color of their skin, the shape of their eyes, or the choice of their partners. Christ still suffers in his members, in those who are falsely accused, victims of injustice, or simply not "cool." Ignacio Ellacuría, the Spanish Jesuit killed with his companions by the Salvadoran military one night in 1989 at the University of Central America in El Salvador, used to speak of the country's poor as *el pueblo crucificado*, "a crucified people." Jon Sobrino, another member of his community who escaped death that night because he was in Bangkok, frequently echoes that phrase in his writings on liberation theology.

The third image comes from the Apostles' Creed. After confessing that Jesus "was crucified, died and was buried" comes this strange verse, "He descended into hell," or as it is sometimes translated, "He descended to the dead." The verse has long puzzled commentators, and even more the faithful. What could it mean?

The image is of Christ going down to the netherworld, to lead out those who had gone before him. An ancient hymn for Holy Saturday pictures Christ descending to free Adam and Eve and their descendants.

Something strange is happening—there is a great silence on earth today, a great silence and stillness....The earth trembled and is still because God has fallen asleep in the flesh and he has raised up all who have slept ever since the world began. God has died in the flesh and hell trembles with fear.

He has gone to search for our first parent, as for a lost sheep. Greatly desiring to visit those who live in darkness and in the shadow of death, he has gone to free from sorrow the captives Adam and Eve, he who is both God and the son of Eve....[And he says,] "Awake, O sleeper, and rise from the dead, and Christ will give you light."[1]

Early Christian literature was familiar with this picture of Christ descending to rescue the righteous. It appears not just in the Apostles' Creed but also in the Athanasian Creed, in some of the apocryphal writings, and in the writings of Melito of Sardis (d. ca. 180), Tertullian (d. 220), Hippolytus (d. ca. 235), Origen (d. ca. 283), and Ambrose (d. 397). The same theme was popular as early as 1000 in Middle English literature and sermons where it was called "the Harrowing of Hell." It appears in Dante's *Inferno*, picturing Jesus descending to free the righteous, all those born from the beginning of the world.

In his beautiful book *The Depth of God's Reach: A Spirituality of Christ's Descent*, Michael Downey provocatively explores this theme. The mystery of Christ's descent, even into hell, shows him entering fully into our human condition, going so far as to die with us and for us. He comes not just for the righteous. His descent into hell, with all its abandonment and despair, is symbolic of God's immeasurable love, which reaches out and embraces even the lost. Downey writes, "The reconciliation of the world was brought about through a complete identification by God with suffering humanity, dying humanity, dead humanity—even those who are thought to be beyond all hope in the clutches of hell."[2]

Downey argues that Christ is united with humanity even in death. The descent is not some stage between Christ's death and the resurrection, but his death, descent, and resurrection are inseparable. His resurrection also is ours, showing the triumph of God's mercy. We find this theme also in the iconography of Eastern Christianity. Christ does not arise from an empty tomb alone but comes forth in glory, surrounded by our ancestors in faith.

Other theologians continue to ponder this mystery of God's love. For Karl Rahner, the doctrine of the incarnation implies God's solidarity not just with the just but with all creation. "Since we are living in the eschaton of Jesus Christ...we know in our Christian faith...the history of salvation as a whole will reach a positive conclusion for the human race through God's own powerful grace."[3] John Thiel suggests that the beloved dead continue Jesus's work of reconciliation, with virtuous action covering the effects of sin lingering in themselves and others, thus contributing to the final realization of God's kingdom.[4]

So here is the final image as we return to that early Christian hymn. Picture Jesus, extending his hand to the sinner, and to each of us, saying, "Awake, O sleeper, and rise from the dead, and Christ will give you life."

9

EASTER

T HE BUNNIES HAVE RETURNED. In the late evening when
I take a brief walk to review the day before retiring, I usually
see a couple of cottontails, watching me carefully in the dark. Thirty
years ago, our lush campus supported many more. One night after
dinner I counted over forty, munching happily on the greenery in
front of our chapel. While sitting quietly after a jog, I would also
occasionally see a fox who had come up to the campus from the
wetlands below. He was not undernourished. But after a while,
the bunnies disappeared, all of them. And shortly afterward, so did
the fox. The last time I saw him, he was very thin, ribs protruding.

Over the centuries the bunny has become a symbol of Easter,
like the tall, white lily (*lilium longiforum*) and colored eggs. Once
called the Easter Rabbit or Easter Hare, the figure originated among
German Lutherans as a mythic figure who determined which children had been good and which had not, not unlike Santa Claus. The
Easter Rabbit would reward the good children with gifts.

For most people today, Easter is a secular feast, not a religious
one, even if Easter Monday is still a holiday in many countries. It is
usually associated with bonnets and fancy dresses, colored eggs, and
baskets of candy brought to children by the Easter Bunny. But the

meaning of the feast is too often forgotten. Few people think of its relation to the liturgical celebration of the resurrection. Easter is not about the bunny; it's about the Lamb.

In the Christian tradition, Jesus is the Lamb of God, who takes away the sins of the world. The image is woven through Scripture. It may go back as far as the mysterious Servant of the Lord, the suffering servant in Isaiah's third "servant song." Isaiah describes him as united with us in his suffering: "He has borne our infirmities and carried our diseases....Like a lamb that is led to the slaughter, and like a sheep that before its shearers is silent, so he did not open his mouth" (Isa 53:4, 7). Saint Paul sees Jesus as the paschal lamb, comparing him to the lamb offered at Passover, celebrating the deliverance of the children of Israel from slavery in Egypt (see 1 Cor 5:7). So too, we are delivered from the slavery of sin. Similarly, the author of the Fourth Gospel sees Jesus as "the Lamb of God who takes away the sin of the world!" (John 1:29).

The image of the Lamb appears over twenty-nine times in the Book of Revelation. In his vision, John the Seer hears of the Lion of Judah who has triumphed, but what he sees in the vision is the Lamb that was slain, the Lamb who triumphs not by force of arms but in dying, his blood purchasing a people from every tribe and nation, that they might be a kingdom and priests to reign on earth. The angels and elders surrounding the throne of God cry out that the Lamb is worthy to receive "power and wealth and wisdom and might and honor and glory and blessing!" from every living creature, forever (Rev 5:12).

In the classic Western liturgy celebrated by Catholics, Anglicans, and Lutherans the image appears again in the *Agnus Dei* or Lamb of God; Jesus is invoked as the one who takes away the sins of the world. The *Agnus Dei* is thought to have been introduced into the Mass by Pope Sergius toward the end of the seventh century. It appears frequently in Christian art as a symbol for Christ. The Lamb holds a standard or banner marked with the cross or sometimes is portrayed resting on a book with seven seals, a reference to the seven seals in Revelation (see Rev 5:5). Often the Lamb pours out its blood, as in the Ghent altarpiece by Jan van Eyck.

Today, some have difficulty finding meaning in the cross. Is there a spirituality connected with it? The Book of Revelation representing Jesus both as the lion of the tribe of Judah and as a lamb suggests an answer. Jesus is portrayed as a lion because of his strength and as a lamb precisely because he triumphs, not through power and violence, but as one "gentle and humble in heart" (Matt 11:29). This paradox is the great mystery of our salvation, the mystery of a God who chooses to renounce power and coercion, signs of the demonic, not of the divine. This is not a powerless God but a kenotic or self-emptying God who, in the words of Pope John Paul II, when faced with human freedom "decided to make Himself 'impotent.'"[1] This is a God who in a certain sense chooses to suffer with us, who in Jesus suffers humiliation and death rather than call upon the hosts of heaven in his own defense. This is a God who leaves the future open, demanding nothing in return, a God who gives himself in love.

Thus, Jesus who entered fully into our humanity knows our vulnerability and pain. He has experienced the injustice that victimizes so many, the violence that destroys lives and communities. His hands, feet, and side still bear his wounds, like our own. Some wounds cannot be seen; they are more existential than physical, wounds from injuries long past but never forgotten. He has those also, Jesus who was abandoned by his friends, stripped naked on the cross, humiliated before the jeering crowd.

But the story of Jesus does not end with the cross. The one he called Abba did not abandon him. God raised him up in glory. His victory over sin and death is the promise of our own. If he still bears his wounds; his woundedness is symbolic of his solidarity with each of us. And his victory will one day be ours. But how do we imagine our risen life?

Jesus's bringing back to life Lazarus or the daughter of the synagogue leader is very different from the resurrection of the body that is our hope. These were resuscitations, bringing back to life someone who had suffered death. It was life restored, not transformed. So the synagogue ruler's little girl became again a lively twelve-year-old, and Lazarus, depending on his age, was restored to his life, with his physical appearance, his aches and pains, whatever wounds he may have carried.

The resurrection of Jesus is something completely different. As Scripture says, the God who raised Jesus from the dead "transform the body of our humiliation that it may be conformed to the body of his glory" (Phil 3:21). But how do we imagine our risen life? What is a glorified body? Christ, the "Last Adam," is the "firstfruits" of the resurrection of the dead; where he has gone, we will one day follow. We can understand this, even if we can't imagine what a risen body will be like.

This question led to considerable speculation by the Church fathers. Tertullian (d. 220) had a rather materialistic understanding of the resurrection; he taught that nothing would be lost, "neither genitals, nor intestines, nor eyelashes, nor toes," while Gregory of Nyssa (d. ca. 395) said the body would rise without age or sex. Augustine (d. 430) held that men would have beards because he felt that beauty was a property of the risen body. In his famous *Sentences* Peter Lombard (d. 1160) pondered the age, height, and sex of those raised, whether they would have fingernails and hair, and how the bodies of those in hell could burn without being consumed.[2]

When Saint Paul tried to describe the life of the resurrection, he spoke of earthly bodies and heavenly bodies, with the latter being a "spiritual body," whatever that means (1 Cor 15:40–44). If the Church fathers could speculate on the nature of the risen body, so also might we. The New Testament suggests that the risen Jesus was no longer bound by the limitations of space and time, and materiality did not at all inhibit his presence to his own, even if the doors were locked. The recurring theme of doubt, fear, and non-recognition on the part of the disciples suggests that the risen body is different, nonobjectifiable. Will materiality itself be in some way transformed, or will our existence be entirely spiritual? Does Einstein's theory of the convertibility of matter and energy offer some clue? Of course, these appearance stories are highly symbolic and are meant to help us, like the first disciples, come to Easter faith.

We can't imagine life after death, but we can understand what it means. Death is not the end. As the Preface of the Mass of Christian Burial proclaims, "for your faithful people, Lord, life is changed not ended, and when this earthly dwelling turns to dust, an eternal dwelling is made ready for them in heaven." Scripture tells us that through Christ's promises we "may come to share in the divine nature, after escaping from the corruption that is in the world" (2 Pet 1:4, NABRE). Certainly, in our risen life we will have memory, otherwise all personal identity would be lost, and the resurrection would not be a personal event. Brian Robinette says suggestively that "resurrection means not dematerialization, but material creation most fully realized."[3]

So too, understanding. Saint Paul tells us we will see God face-to-face: "Now I know only in part; then I will know fully, even as I have been fully known" (1 Cor 13:12; see 1 John 3:2). Heaven entails our union with God. Yet according to Aquinas, even in the beatific vision God remains mystery, beyond our ability to comprehend. Still there is a trinitarian dimension to the beatific vision, for our union with God is to encounter God as Father, Son, and Spirit.[4] Our ability to understand is already a participation in the uncreated light of the divine; what will it be when we share fully in that light?

If relationality is at the heart of the Trinity and, as Pope Francis insists, we grow in holiness to the extent that we enter into communion with God, others, and all creation, then our share in the fullness of the divine life suggests that our ability to gather in communion with one another will be enhanced, not diminished. We anticipate that communion in Christ's Body, the Church, and in the Eucharist that unites us with Christ and with one another. And we long for the day when we will be reunited with our beloved dead. As Joseph Ratzinger has said, "Eternal life does not isolate a person, but leads him out of isolation into true unity, with his brothers and sisters and the whole of God's creation."[5]

This is the mystery we celebrate at the great Easter Vigil, when we gather before the darkened church to enkindle and bless the paschal candle, symbol of the risen Christ who gives his light to the world. As that new light is shared with all those present, the deacon chants the joyous Easter hymn, the Exultet, calling on the hosts of heaven and the angels to rejoice at "our mighty King's triumph." The hymn goes on to celebrate Christ's breaking the bonds of death and rising victorious from the underworld, turning the night into the brightness of day, washing our faults away and restoring innocence to the fallen. In the concluding verse we pray,

Therefore, O Lord,
we pray that this candle,
hallowed to the honor of your name,
may persevere undimmed,
to overcome the darkness of this night.
Receive it as a pleasing fragrance,
and let it mingle with the lights of heaven.
May this flame be found still burning
by the Morning Star:

CHRIST AND HIS BODY

the one Morning Star who never sets,
Christ your Son,
who, coming back from death's domain,
has shed his peaceful light on humanity,
and lives and reigns for ever and ever,
Amen.

10

DO WE NEED THE CHURCH?

O NE OF THE QUESTIONS often heard today is why do we need the Church? The disaffiliation of so many from institutional religion is one of the phenomena of our time. It continues to increase. A 2020 Gallup poll indicated that only 47 percent of Americans said they belonged to a church, synagogue, or mosque. A 2021 Pew Research Center study reveals that roughly half of Black adults raised Catholic, 54 percent, still so identify. The loss of young adult Catholics is particularly significant. Not only are many leaving the Church; many come from families no longer practicing the faith.

The pervasive secularism of our culture is certainly one of the reasons for the decline. There are few cultural supports for religious practice. The media is relentlessly secular. The banishment of the transcendent has led to its spurious reappearance in multiple films about zombies, vampires, superheroes, time travel, and ersatz supernaturalisms. Many young people identify conservative Christianity with regressive right-wing politics, often through its own fault. In 2020, 81 percent of white evangelicals voted for Donald

Trump, along with 57 percent of white Catholics, while overall, Biden received 52 percent of the Catholic vote.

Catholics are certainly affected by these trends. But there are other reasons as well for departures from the Church, among them the sexual abuse scandal, clericalism, and what James Keenan calls "hierarchicalism," a privileged status for bishops insulating them from accountability to those they are supposed to serve.[1] Many young people have difficulty with Church teaching on women and gays. And there are other issues that need to be address. So the Church is not without some responsibility.

The clergy sexual abuse crisis has been described as the greatest crisis facing the Catholic Church since the Reformation in the sixteenth century. When cases of sexual abuse first became public in the mid-1980s, the bishops were slow to respond. They sent offending priests off for treatment, only to learn that psychological interventions were insufficient when many offended again. With pressure from the faithful and especially the media, the bishops were finally forced to take more significant action. In 2002, after a meeting in Dallas, they put in place a "Charter for the Protection of Children and Young People," known as the Dallas Charter. It called for "zero tolerance" for any priest or church minister credibly accused of abusing a minor, permanently removing them from ministry. Unfortunately, there were no sanctions for bishops who failed to deal with them.

Rome was even slower in responding. Some in the Vatican tended to dismiss the crisis as "an American problem."[2] One of the first to deal with it was Pope Benedict XVI, though he too had failed to act decisively while archbishop of Munich-Freising (1977–1982). As head of the Congregation for the Doctrine of the Faith, he centralized procedures for dealing with accused priests and streamlined processes for dismissing them from ministry. Shortly after his election to the papacy, he removed from office and remanded to a life of prayer and penance Mexican Father Marcial Maciel, founder of the Legionaries of Christ, long accused of abusing several of the Legion's seminarians. Studies of abuse began in Ireland in 1990; since then, they have appeared in Australia (2017), Germany (2018), and the Netherlands (2018), among others, adding thousands to the global list of victims. Even Pope Francis was embarrassed when, in 2015, he appointed Juan Barros a bishop in Chile over the objections of several other Chilean bishops for failing to deal with a popular priest forced into retirement because of abusing children. In responding, he called all the country's bishops to Rome and accepted the resignations of eight of them.

Francis finally acted decisively to address the issue globally. After calling the heads of the world's episcopal conferences to Rome in 2019, his *motu proprio*, *Vos estis lux mundi*, put in place new procedural rules to combat abuse and to ensure that bishops and religious superiors be held accountable for their actions. It mandated clerics to report cases of clerical sexual abuse to church authorities and to follow laws about reporting to civil authorities. The sexual abuse crisis has damaged beyond measure thousands of young people. Though the Church is not the only institution guilty of this sin, it is especially damaging when done by those considered trustworthy and representing the holy.

Not unrelated to the sexual abuse crisis is clericalism, an enduring culture that treats the ordained as a superior, privileged class, refusing to recognize the dignity of the baptized. Pope Francis has continued to denounce it. In 2018, his Letter to the People of God linked the two: "To say 'no' to abuse is to say an emphatic 'no' to all forms of clericalism." He sees clericalism as

> an approach that "not only nullifies the character of
> Christians, but also tends to diminish and undervalue
> the baptismal grace that the Holy Spirit has placed in the

heart of our people." Clericalism, whether fostered by priests themselves or by lay persons, leads to an excision in the ecclesial body that supports and helps to perpetuate many of the evils that we are condemning today.[3]

Some priests find it difficult to work with lay ministers as partners, claiming a superior status, an "ontological difference" based on ordination. This not only represents an abuse of authority; it also exhibits a theological failure to acknowledge that all men and women share equally in the Church's mission in virtue of their baptism. Clericalism remains a problem, despite Francis's efforts to address it.

A similar problem is felt by many Catholics in second marriages who are looking for understanding and compassion, not an annulment process that seems legalistic and often painful. Pope Francis sought to address this after the two Synods of Bishops on the family (2014–2015) with his apostolic letter *Amoris laetitia*. Keenan uses the slowness of so many archbishops to establish programs implementing the pope's teaching in the letter as another example of hierarchicalism. Of the thirty-two archdioceses in the United States, twenty had little on their websites but brief news references about the pope's letter. Keenan calls this "*Amoris*-light."[4]

While our secular culture makes living a life of faith difficult, the Church could do more to improve its evangelical and catechetical ministries. Many adults today are poorly schooled in their faith. Most young Catholics grow up in non-Catholic schools. Nor does the Church best reach those in Catholic schools by basing their religious education on the *Catechism of the Catholic Church*. The *Catechism* is a useful compendium of Catholic doctrine; many Protestants wish they had a similar volume. But young people don't need to memorize doctrines; they need an evangelical approach that speaks to their experience. Many find the Church's inability to fully accept gay people and to include women in all its ministries deeply troubling. Not a few who join other churches complain that Catholicism has not helped them find a relationship with God. And they need teachers, mentors, and friends who can share their own faith experience with them. Catholic pastors, teachers, and theologians continue to struggle to find a language to present the good news of the gospel in their ministry, especially to the young and to others who have moved beyond its community.

We are essentially social creatures. Without relationships—family, friends, teachers, society—we cannot develop as persons. Language, self-consciousness, a sense of identity—all are socially mediated. Catholicism's fundamental ethos is communitarian, not individualistic. Nor can one be a Christian all by oneself, disconnected from a community of faith.

We do not encounter God directly, in some inner experience, exterior vision, or theological formulae. While we can encounter the divine in our experience, it is always an experience mediated by symbols: persons, events, biblical texts, rituals, or nature itself. But these symbols are not self-explanatory and can be misconstrued. They are expressed in human language, which is always historically and culturally conditioned. They become revelatory only within an interpretative community. That is why we need the Church.

While Saint Paul is often seen as an example of a religious individualist, teaching salvation by faith alone, his epistles are strongly ecclesiological. For Paul, to be "in Christ" is to be in his Body, the Church. His letters are always to or about churches. He tells us that we are baptized in the Spirit into one Body (see 1 Cor 12:13), made the one Body of Christ through sharing in the one bread of the Eucharist (1 Cor 10:16–17), incorporated into a community with different gifts (*charismata*) and ministries. The Church is not primarily an institution; it is an assembly of those called out (*ekklesia*), a community of disciples. Without the Church, we cannot encounter

Christ. The Church brings us into relationship with Christ, mediating his presence in Scripture, sacramental symbols, worship, and those who touch others through their faith, goodness, or compassionate service.

Scripture always needs to be interpreted. It has its origins in cultures and languages very different from our own. Divorced from the historical community that lives from its witness, interprets it within its living tradition, and celebrates it liturgically, the Scriptures can easily be misinterpreted. It needs a context. It cannot stand as an independent source. The Reformation principle of *Scriptura sui interpres*, Scripture interprets itself, collapsed with modernity and the historical-critical method.[5] Similarly, without a living tradition, sacraments can easily become empty rituals rather than an encounter with grace. Theology also, when removed from the living faith of the historical Christian community, can easily become abstract speculation or collapse into a fundamentalist or political ideology.

The Christian tradition also has a more popular expression in catechetical texts, Christian art, its charitable works, spirituality, mysticism, and the lives of its saints. Symbols are powerful; they appeal not just to the head but also to the heart, to our affectivity and imagination. We inhabit symbols, and they can transform us; they put us in touch with the mystery of the Divine. Andrew Greeley was accustomed to distinguishing between the "high tradition" expressed in the teaching of theologians and the Church's magisterium—a doctrinal, cognitive Catholicism—and the "popular tradition" handed on by parents, teachers, and friends—a more imaginative, poetic, affective Catholicism. While both are important, he argues that "the popular tradition has so much more raw power and immediacy" for people's lives.[6] It is for this same reason that Pope Francis prefers popular religiosity or the *teología del pueblo* of Latin America, rooted in the devotional life of the people, over a more theoretical, European liberation theology.[7]

So, why do we need the Church? We need the Church because Christianity grows out of what scholars today refer to as the Jesus movement, a call to men and women to join with him in proclaiming the reign of God, a message of healing, hope, and good news for the poor (see Luke 4:18–19). We can't be Christians all by ourselves; the Church proclaims a gospel that has an intrinsically social dimension. The Church continues to celebrate Christ's presence among his own, to hand on the Jesus story in word and sacrament, to witness to the reign in works of charity and justice. There are lessons to be learned from history.

Is it also a sinful Church? Yes, although official Catholicism does not tend to use this language because it recognizes the Church as holy, the presence of God's grace in Christ's body, in the Scriptures, the sacraments, and the communion of saints. But if the Church is sinful, so also is the human community.

Even if the story of the Fall in Genesis is a myth, like most myths, it teaches an important lesson. Our first parents were living an idyllic existence in the Garden of Eden. The serpent's temptation to eat the forbidden fruit is subtle; it is a temptation not to evil but to something good, to knowledge. "God knows that when you eat of it your eyes will be opened, and you will be like God, knowing good and evil" (Gen 3:5). But what it conceals is the fundamental temptation that lies at the root of all sin, to become gods ourselves, taking the place of the one who alone is God. In a commentary on this passage, Stephen Duffy says that the man and woman fall "because they are capable of reaching for the stars, seeking divine status and becoming the source of their own meaning."[8] We can reach for the stars. But we can also fall from grace. That is why we need the Church.

11

THE BODY AND
BLOOD OF CHRIST?

DURING THEIR LONG WANDERING out of Egypt, the children of Israel grumbled against Moses in the desert because they were hungry. Why did you lead us into this desert to die of hunger, when in Egypt "we sat by the fleshpots and ate our fill of bread" (Exod 16:3)? But God was not absent. God gave them bread from heaven, the manna that nourished them on their journey. In John's Gospel, the author picks up on this story in chapter 6, all of which is eucharistic.

The chapter begins with the story of Jesus multiplying the loaves and two fish to feed the hungry crowd that was following him. In the Synoptic Gospels, the same story is told twice, in both Matthew and Mark, using a version of the eucharistic formula still used in the celebration to the Mass: "Taking the seven loaves he gave thanks, broke them, and gave them to his disciples to distribute" (Mark 8:6, NABRE). In John's Gospel, after the story of Jesus walking on the water to join his disciples in the boat comes the great "Bread of Life" discourse. When the crowd joins Jesus and the disciples the next day across the sea, they remind him of how their ancestors ate bread in the desert. Jesus responds that he is the true bread from heaven, the bread of life to give life to the world. Like their fathers in the desert with Moses, the people grumble or murmur, asking how Jesus can say he has come down from heaven. At this point, the metaphor of the bread from heaven refers to Jesus and his teaching.

But there is a transition at verse 6:51, where Jesus again refers to himself as the living bread come down from heaven, but then says that whoever eats this bread will live forever. The passage becomes explicitly eucharistic: "Those who eat my flesh and drink my blood have eternal life, and I will raise them up on the last day; for my flesh is true food and my blood is true drink. Those who eat my flesh and drink my blood abide in me, and I in them" (John 6:54–56). This is too much for the bystanders to accept. Not just those in the crowd, but some of the disciples leave his company. When Jesus asks the Twelve if they too want to leave, the chapter ends with these beautiful words of Simon Peter: "Lord, to whom can we go? You have the words of eternal life. We have come to believe and know that you are the Holy One of God" (John 6:68–69). Peter's confession of faith here is the Johannine version of his confession of Jesus as the Messiah at Caesarea Philippi in the Synoptic tradition.

While the Bread of Life discourse represents the eucharistic faith of the early Christian communities rather than an actual discourse of the historical Jesus during his ministry, it serves as evidence of the centrality of the Eucharist from the early days of the Church. The Eucharist has always been at the center of our Catholic life and worship. The great eucharistic prayer praises and thanks God for the life, death, resurrection of Jesus, the gift of the Spirit, and his promise to come again to gather us to himself. Receiving the bread blessed and the cup poured out gives us intimate union with the risen Jesus and unites us as the Body of Christ for the world. For this reason, we call it "holy communion." Saint Ignatius of Loyola held the Eucharist with such great reverence that he waited for a year after his ordination before celebrating it for the first time. Unfortunately, like the bystanders in John's narrative, many no longer walk with us today.

When our churches were closed during the COVID-19 pandemic and we could not gather for Mass, I was moved by the hunger so many expressed for the Eucharist. I had friends, both near and far, who spent considerable time searching for an online liturgy that would nourish their faith, and when they found one, they would tune in faithfully every Sunday. Still, our bishops are rightly concerned about a diminished understanding of Christ's eucharistic presence and about a reduced participation in the sacramental celebration.

So, what do we understand by the Eucharist? I'm not sure that the lack of understanding of the eucharistic mystery is as widespread as some think. The survey most often referenced concerns belief in the Real Presence that was conducted by the Pew Research Center.[1] In my judgment, its questions were not carefully formulated and hence are ambiguous. It reports that 69 percent of Catholics surveyed say they believe that the bread and wine used in the Mass "are symbols of the body and blood of Jesus Christ." That is not necessarily incorrect.

If they mean that they are *only* symbols, without Christ's real presence, it would replicate the mistake of the eleventh-century theologian and head of the school of Saint Martin at Tours, Berengarius (d. 1088), who seems to have taught that Christ was present in the bread and wine *only* as sign, thus a merely symbolic presence. In response, the Council of Rome (1059) required him to confess that the bread and wine placed on the altar after consecration are "not only a sacrament but also the true body and blood of our Lord Jesus Christ, and with the senses not only sacramentally but in truth are taken and broken by the hands of the priests and crushed by the teeth of the faithful."[2] This confession seems to us today as overly literal; as David Power says, "Who today would care to state that communicants chew on the body of Christ?"[3] Martin Luther used similar language. Karl Rahner speaks of sacraments as "real symbols," symbols that mediate or make present the reality they symbolize.

The Pew Forum survey also reports that 31 percent of Catholics say that they believe that "the bread and wine actually become the body and blood of Jesus." But this also can be misinterpreted. It could represent an overly literal understanding of Christ's presence. The eucharistic bread is not "literally" or "physically" Christ's body, and the consecrated wine is not literally or physically his blood, as we so often read in articles about the controversy. When I ask students: When you receive only the eucharistic bread, are you receiving only the body of Christ? Many answer yes. This, of course, is incorrect.

The Fourth Lateran Council (1215) adopted the term *transubstantiation* in response to Berengarius to safeguard the Church's eucharistic faith. The sixteenth-century Council of Trent used it again as an "appropriate" (*aptissime*) way of talking about what happens in the Eucharist. It affirmed that the substance of the bread and wine are changed in the Eucharist into the substance of Christ's body and blood, while the appearances ("species") of the bread and wine remain the same.

But more importantly, the Council affirmed that in the Eucharist the whole Christ was present, "body and blood, soul and divinity" (DS 1651). In other words, what is present is not discrete flesh and blood, but the risen Jesus himself in his glorified humanity. The *Catechism of the Catholic Church* adopts this more appropriate language of Trent: In the Eucharist, "the body and blood, together with the soul and divinity, of our Lord Jesus Christ and therefore, *the whole Christ is truly, really, and substantially* contained" (§1374).

Transubstantiation is a philosophical term, very different from the language of the New Testament, which speaks of encountering the risen Jesus in the meal. We do better in starting with the meal. Paul tells us that the cup of blessing in the Eucharist gives us a participation or communion (*koinonia*) in the blood of Christ, the bread broken gives us a participation or communion in the body of Christ (see 1 Cor 10:16); Luke speaks of the disciples on the road to Emmaus recognizing the risen Jesus in the breaking of the bread (see Luke 24:31, 35). John's language is more literal; Jesus says, "unless you eat the flesh of the Son of Man and drink his blood, you have no life in you" (John 6:53), but the reference is still to a meal. Gradually, a more literal understanding developed, speaking of a change of the elements, but it was not the only way of expressing the mystery.

Does the risen Jesus literally have flesh and blood? How do we understand the nature of the risen body? Saint Paul struggled to understand Christ's glorified humanity in 1 Corinthians, but his language breaks down when he tries to describe it. He calls it a spiritual body, speaking of the risen Jesus, "the last Adam," as a life-giving spirit (1 Cor 15:45). It remains a mystery, one that fascinated many of the Church fathers and medieval theologians, as we saw earlier.

Perhaps the later development of the doctrine of the Trinity might provide insight here. The doctrine of the Trinity is an articulation of what is revealed of God—Father, Son, and Spirit. On that basis, reflection turns to what is often thought of as the "inner" or eternal life of God: three persons, diverse in mission, one in being. In receiving the Eucharist, the risen Christ, Son and Word of the Father, no longer bound by space and time, comes to dwell in us, uniting us with himself and with one another in his body, the Church. It is not enough for contemporary Catholics simply to repeat the formulas of the past.

In receiving holy communion, we truly receive the risen Christ who gives himself to us as food and drink, his body and blood. As Nathan Mitchell has said so well, "The body of Christ offered to Christians in consecrated bread and wine is not some-*thing* but some*one*."[4] It is the living Jesus we encounter, who gives us intimate communion with himself and participation in the life of the triune God.

PART III

PRAYER
AND
WORSHIP

12

MARKED BY THE CROSS

H OW OFTEN HAVE WE SEEN a character in a film at some
crucial, often life-threatening moment make the Sign of
the Cross? Right away we suspect the person is supposed to be a
Catholic. The Sign of the Cross is the unique symbol of Catholic
faith. As it is for Anglicans, Episcopalians, and the Orthodox,
though Orthodox Christians bless themselves from right to left,
rather from left to right as the others do. For some, the Sign of the
Cross can seem more like a superstitious ritual, like blessing oneself
before a free-throw in a basketball game.

But the cross of Jesus is one of the oldest symbols of Christian faith. Thus, Paul wrote to the Galatians, "May I never boast
of anything except the cross of our Lord Jesus Christ" (Gal 6:14),
or to the Corinthians, "The message about the cross is foolishness
to those who are perishing, but to us who are being saved it is the
power of God" (1 Cor 1:18). Christians have blessed themselves
with the Sign of the Cross since the earliest days. According to
Tertullian (d. 220),

> In all our travels and movements, in all our coming in
> and going out, in putting on our shoes, at the bath, at

the table, in lighting our candles, in lying down, in sitting down, whatever employment occupies us, we mark our foreheads with the sign of the cross. (*De corona* 30)

Similarly, Saint Cyril of Jerusalem (d. 386) stated,

Let us then not be ashamed to confess the Crucified. Be the cross our seal, made with boldness by our fingers on our brow and in everything; over the bread we eat and the cups we drink, in our comings in and in our goings out; before our sleep, when we lie down and when we awake; when we are in the way, and when we are still. (*Catechetical Lecture* 13)

If, however, the cross is a symbol of Christ's victory over sin and death, it should not be made the unique instrument of our redemption, a necessary sacrifice. Eastern theology has most often stressed the transformation of the human through the incarnation, often expressed as divinization (*theosis*). The theology of the Western Church, influenced by the practicality of the Roman Empire, with its commercial and legal culture, too often described salvation as a transaction, some kind of price paid by Christ by his bloody death to atone for our sins or make satisfaction for Adam's offense against divine justice.

Many of the early Church fathers, both East and West, used the images of a "ransom" offered to the devil or a sacrifice to God to explain Christ's death. For Irenaeus (d. 200), Christ's death was a ransom paid to the devil to set us free from the power of sin. Tertullian sees Christ's death as the reason for his birth. Origen (d. ca. 254) also spoke of a ransom paid to the devil, as well as employing the images of sacrifice and propitiation. Athanasius (d. 373) used similar language, but he also saw the incarnation as a restoration of humanity to its original state, a re-creation. Gregory of Nyssa (d. ca. 395) uses the image of God offering Jesus as a ransom, overcoming the devil like a fish caught by bait concealing a hook. Augustine (d. 430) uses several images. He sees Christ's death as a ransom paid to the devil into whose power humankind had fallen because of sin, comparing it this time to a mouse caught in a trap. He also uses the language of sacrifice, a "propitiation" making satisfaction for our sins.

But it was Anselm of Canterbury (d. 1109) who was to give definitive form to this "atonement" theology. His famous book, *Cur Deus Homo?* ("Why Did God Become Man?"), argues that Adam's sin was an infinite offense because it was against the infinite justice of God, and therefore only an infinite being could make the satisfaction needed to cancel the offense. For this reason, God became human. From this came the theology of "substitutionary atonement," sometimes called "penal satisfaction," the idea that Jesus suffered the punishment due our sins. This has become one of the five fundamentals of evangelical theology. If evangelical Christianity has canonized Anselm's theology, it still surfaces in Catholic theology and is expressed frequently in the 2011 translation of the Roman Missal, the text for the official Catholic liturgy.

Here is a case where we must be careful with our theological language. God did not require the sacrifice of his only beloved son to bring us saving grace. The offense against his justice that was Adam's sin did not require satisfaction. Even the Jewish Scriptures moved beyond the idea of blood sacrifices as pleasing to God. In Psalms we read,

> Do I eat the flesh of bulls
> or drink the blood of goats?
> Offer to God a sacrifice of thanksgiving,
> and pay your vows to the Most High. (Ps 50:13–14)

Or in Hosea,

> For I desire steadfast love and not sacrifice,
>   the knowledge of God rather than burnt offerings.
>   (Hos 6:6)

In the institution narrative or "words of consecration" used in the Eucharist, Jesus speaks of "my body which will be given up for you" and of "the chalice of my blood…which will be poured out for you and for many for the forgiveness of sins." The biblical language is, of course, metaphorical.

It was not just the death of Jesus that brought about a saving relationship with the Father; it is the whole Christ event that saves us: his life, death, resurrection, and gift of the Spirit, giving us communion in the divine life. Jesus shows us the way to the Father and enables us with grace. He is "the way, and the truth, and the life" (John 14:6). Thus, the mystery of the incarnation is more than the nativity. Our redemption is not some "second step" after Adam and Eve ruined God's plan, so to speak, through their sin. Creation is God's work through the Word and in the Spirit. Original sin is an important doctrine, too easily dismissed. But if creation is "fallen," it is also graced. Saving grace, God's self-communication, is offered to all, not just to those who follow Jesus (*LG* 16). But not all respond. God always respects our freedom.

Jesus's ministry began with his proclaiming the reign of God. As he gathered a group of disciples around him—the Jesus "movement," as it is called by theologians today—they joined with him in his ministry. He sent them out to heal the sick, cleanse lepers, drive out demons, proclaim that the kingdom of God is at hand, and raise the dead (Matt 10:7–8; Luke 10:9). The Beatitudes reflect God's special concern for the last and the least that played such an important part in Jesus's preaching and was to inform the ministry of the disciples. He taught them to refrain from judging or condemning others, to share what they have, to love their enemies. They were to be merciful, like God who is merciful.

Jesus died because his mission of proclaiming the reign of God, with its "glad tidings" for the poor (Luke 4:18), was offensive to some of the religious leaders of his day. Even more, he outraged the chief priests and scribes by proclaiming that the Temple would be destroyed (see Mark 13:1–2), symbolizing its destruction by driving out those who changed coins and sold the small animals necessary for sacrificial offerings, in effect closing down the Temple cult for failing to bear fruit (see Mark 11:15–17). This is a point Mark underlines by bookending the "temple cleansing" with the story of Jesus cursing the unfruitful fig tree.

Jesus was faithful to his mission to proclaim the nearness of God's reign, even at the cost of his life. His death is the price he paid for his fidelity, the sacrifice that represents the total gift of himself to that mission, symbolic of God's love for all people. It shows the Son of God vulnerable before evil and injustice, like so many of his brothers and sisters, Jesus who renounced power and refused to turn to violence, submitting, as Scripture says, like a lamb led to the slaughter or a sheep before the shearers (see Isa 53:7). Obedient unto death, even to death on the cross, his death was a prelude to God raising him up to everlasting life.

The saving work of Jesus is carried on by the Church in the power of the Spirit that raised Jesus from the dead. When Pope Francis writes that "the task of 'taking up the cross' becomes participating with Christ in the salvation of the world,"[1] he underlines the solidarity of the disciples in Christ's saving mission. Theology calls this the paschal mystery, and Saint Paul tells us that we should have the same attitude ourselves (see Phil 2:5). Jesus lived in complete union with God, whom he called Abba, Father. Though reviled by others, he remained gracious. Though tempted, he did not sin.

His whole life was one of seeking not his own will but the will of the One who sent him, proclaiming the reign of God even when it became evident that the opposition his preaching occasioned would eventually cost him his life. We manifest the pattern of the paschal mystery by living as he did, united with the Father, in life and in death.

Paul tells us that at our baptisms, we are baptized into his death, that we might also share in his resurrection (see Rom 6:3–4). In the Rite of Christian Burial, these words will be repeated when our body is brought to the church for the funeral liturgy. We are told repeatedly in the Gospels to pick up our own cross and come after him.

Salvation remains God's work in Christ Jesus. Creation and salvation are not two acts but one. Creation begins, is graced, is sustained, and reaches its fullness in and through the Word. But Jesus, the Word made flesh, joins our labors to his own. We join our sacrifices in solidarity with his; we witness to God's reign, so that others might come to experience it, taking up our crosses, so that we might follow him. In the Letter to the Hebrews, Jesus is seen as high priest by offering his life and death; in solidarity with him we have become his brothers and sisters, even his "partners" (Heb 3:14).

So, Jesus's own work is carried on by his disciples, united by baptism and the Eucharist into his Body, the Church. In its preaching, its teaching, its liturgy, its communion or fellowship, and its ministry the Church makes visible Christ at work in the world. There is a strongly social dimension to the Church's ministry. Catholics of another generation knew by heart the Corporal Works of Mercy and tried to put them into practice: to feed the hungry, give drink to the thirsty, shelter the homeless, visit the sick or imprisoned, ransom the captive, and bury the dead.

The Church has a rich tradition of social teaching, though many Catholics today are unfamiliar with it.[2] Ignacio Ellacuría, rector at the

Jesuit University of San Salvador, sought to give expression to the Church's social teaching in the research, publications, and teaching of his university. Writing from his experience of El Salvador's suffering people, he used a powerful metaphor, saying that we are called to take the crucified peoples of the world down from their cross.[3] But this is a costly work; it cost Ellacuría and his companions their lives. Pope Francis has used similar language. He writes that the Church was born in the margins of the cross, where so many of the crucified are to be found. Our evangelization should begin here, with the poor at the margins, at the edges, not from the center. "The road to the geographic and existential margins is the route of the Incarnation: God chose the peripheries as the place to reveal, in Jesus, His saving action in history."[4]

Thus, for Catholics and other Christians, not just the cross, but the crucifix with the corpus of Jesus has long served as the symbol of their faith. It is so much more than an ornament or piece of jewelry. Jesus's ministry was to show us the way to the One he called Father. A living example of God's compassion, he healed the sick, drove out evil spirts, and proclaimed good news to the poor. When his ministry aroused the opposition of political and religious leaders, he accepted his fate, placing himself in his Father's hands. If we are his friends and disciples, we can do no less.

13

SPIRITUAL SACRIFICES

INTROÍBO AD ALTÁRE DEI. Ad Deum qui lætíficat juventútem meam. As a boy serving at the altar, I had to learn this Latin dialogue between the priest and the server, which opened the Mass in those days before Vatican II. In English, "I will go to the altar of God," and the response, "To the God who brings joy to my youth." The God who brings joy to my youth; those words have stayed with me over the years and have touched something within me. But their precise sentiment has been lost in our current translation, no longer based on Jerome's Vulgate. Still, they point to something real.

Some liturgists insist we call the altar a table. We all love a meal with family or dear friends, made more intimate with candles or a fine wine. Such a meal is a sign of communion. When we gather to celebrate the Lord's Supper, the meal that sustains us as Christians, we are united into the Body of Christ (see 1 Cor 10:16–17). This sacramental meal also anticipates the great eschatological banquet with good food and fine wines, foretold in the Jewish Scriptures (see Isa 55:1–2; Prov 9:1–5) and in Matthew's image of the great wedding feast (see Matt 8:11; 22:1–14).

From the Church's earliest days Christians have gathered on the Lord's Day to break bread and share the cup in memory of

Jesus, proclaiming his death until he comes again (see 1 Cor 11:23–32), recognizing him in the breaking of the bread (see Luke 24:31, 35). In the Letter to the Ephesians, the author reminds the people of the will of the Lord, "as you sing psalms and hymns and spiritual songs among yourselves, singing and making melody to the Lord in your hearts, giving thanks to God the Father at all times and for everything in the name of our Lord Jesus Christ" (Eph 5:19–20). Here we see a community gathered in prayer and worship. They did so on Sunday, the day Christ rose from the dead.[1] Our eucharistic language—bread from heaven, the bread of life, the body and blood of Jesus, "holy communion," the most holy sacrament of the altar—is rich indeed and suggestive.

In Catholic theology, the Eucharist is also a sacrifice, a memorial (*anamnesis*) of the sacrifice of Christ, expressed in the eucharistic words at the Last Supper. "This is my body, which will be given for you.... This cup is the new covenant in my blood, which will be shed for you" (Luke 22:19–20, NABRE). Many Catholics still refer to the Eucharist as "the holy sacrifice of the Mass." As a memorial of Christ's sacrifice, the term *altar* is still appropriate.

Thus, the mystery of the Eucharist has many dimensions; like a diamond, it is multifaceted. Not merely a sacramental meal, it is also the Church's great prayer of thanksgiving (*eucharistia*), giving the sacrament its name. It is a memorial of the sacrifice of Christ, an invocation of the Holy Spirit, and a sign of the kingdom, gathering people of every race and tribe and nation into the one Body of Christ.

To gather around the altar is to enter into the holy; we dwell in the intersection of heaven and earth. In the ancient Roman Canon, now the First Eucharistic Prayer, we remember Christ's passion, death, resurrection, and ascension to the Father, praying "that all of us who through this participation at the altar receive the most holy Body and Blood of your Son may be filled with every grace and heavenly blessing." Eastern Orthodox Christians see what they call the "Divine Liturgy" as a participation in the heavenly liturgy of praise and worship, standing in the very presence of God. We do this also, introducing the great Sanctus acclamation that concludes the Preface, with words such as "and so with Angels and Archangels, with Thrones and Dominions, and with all the hosts and Powers of heaven, we sing the hymn of your glory, as without end we acclaim."

In his apostolic exhortation on the Eucharist, *Sacramentum caritatis*, Pope Benedict XVI emphasized that active participation means more than simply taking different roles in the celebration. We need to enter into the celebration intentionally, not just with our bodies, but with our minds and hearts. We participate actively by having a conscious awareness of the mystery of the Eucharist and the great prayer that rises to the Father and how it relates to our daily life (*SC* 48). Benedict cites Vatican II's Constitution on the Sacred Liturgy, *Sacrosanctum concilium*, calling for the faithful to join in "offering the Immaculate Victim, not only through the hands of the priest, but also with him, they should learn also to offer themselves; through Christ the Mediator, they should be drawn day by day into ever more perfect union with God and with each other, so that finally God may be all in all" (*SC* 48).

In a remarkable phrase, Saint Paul speaks of his own sufferings as "completing what is lacking in Christ's afflictions for the sake of his body, that is, the church...to make the word of God fully known, the mystery that has been hidden throughout the ages" (Col 1:24–26). The author of 1 Peter exhorts the Christians of Asia Minor to see themselves as called "to be a holy priesthood, to offer spiritual sacrifices acceptable to God through Jesus Christ" (1 Pet 2:5). The reference is to what is called today the "baptismal" or "common" priesthood, the share of all the baptized in the one priesthood of Christ (see *LG* 10, 34), calling all to offer spiritual sacrifices, joining their sacrifices in union with the Father to that of Jesus. If this text is rarely cited by official sources, it should be recognized that it was very important to Saint Augustine. In *The City of God*, he said that "every work that effects our union with God in a holy fellowship is a true sacrifice....As a consequence, even that mercy by which aid is given to man is not a sacrifice unless it is done for the sake of God" (*City of God* 10.6).

Catholics in an earlier age had a clearer sense of joining their sacrifices to that of Christ, linking their lives and service of others with his sacrifice. As children, when faced with little sacrifices we were encouraged to "offer it up," or, as I remember, "offer it up for the starving Armenians." But we need to be careful of our language here.

Jesus's death was not something God's justice demanded, nor was it a ransom paid to the devil, as some metaphorical language of the Church fathers suggests, as we saw earlier. Jesus offered his ministry, his life, even his death, the result of the offense taken by some who were threatened by his preaching. His whole life was lived in union with God. This was his sacrifice, as Augustine describes it above. When we join our good works and our sufferings to his, we join in his salvific work.

I've always been greatly moved by what Edith Stein, now known as Saint Teresa Benedicta of the Cross, said to her sister Rosa when the Gestapo came to take them from the Carmelite convent in Echt, in the Netherlands, where they had taken refuge. As they began their terrible journey to the East, she said, "Come, Rosa, we're going for our people." Saint Teresa Benedicta had a clear sense of joining their sacrifice to that of Jesus. They died at Auschwitz on August 9, 1942.[2]

Discussing the redemptive value of sacrificial love, Russian Orthodox Metropolitan Anthony Bloom tells of a prayer on a scrap of wrapping paper found after the war in a concentration camp, written by one of the men who perished there. It read:

> Lord, when you come as a Judge of the earth, do not condemn the people who have done such atrocious things to us; do not hold against them their cruelty and our suffering, their violence and our despair, but look at the fruits which we have borne in patience, in humility, in fortitude, in forgiveness, in loyalty, in solidarity; and may these fruits be accounted unto their salvation. Do not allow the memory of us to be in eternity a horror to them; may it be their salvation.[3]

This generous prayer surely reflects a moment of grace, as do the prayers left behind by two Christians killed in Lebanon's bloody civil war that broke out in 1975.

Shortly after his ordination in 1973, Fr. Nicolas Kluiters, a Dutch Jesuit, was sent to Lebanon where he spent ten years in the Northern Beqaa Valley, working for social and economic development. When a good friend and catechist, Ghassibé Keyrouz, was murdered, his family found a will in his room, asking them to forgive those who killed him and offering his blood for peace and harmony in Lebanon.

For his safety, Fr. Kluiters's superiors called him back to Europe; he was sent to Belgium for his Tertianship, or "Third Year" of formation. Afterward, fully aware of the danger he would face, he returned to the Beqaa Valley to resume his work. In 1985, after a few months in Rome for a spirituality course, he returned to Lebanon. On March 13, he left the village of Hermel for a meeting with representatives of the Order of Malta who supported his mission. He never arrived. His tortured body was found on April 1 at the bottom of a deep chasm, not far from where his friend Ghassibé had been found. And like the case of his friend, after Fr. Kluiters's death, this prayer, handwritten in Arabic, was found in his room:

> *God, Holy Father, I offer you my life for the salvation of my Muslim brothers and for the salvation of the people of the whole world. Receive my offering with the sacrifice of the body and blood of Jesus for the glory of your name. I offer it to you for my brothers, the poor and all the oppressed, so that they may discover in the justice and love of Christ the path to true libera-tion. I offer it to you for all believers so that the unity of faith may be restored among them. I offer it to you so that all people may respect each other and recognize that there will always and everywhere be differences in character and generations, and thus overcome any preference for one class over another, for one people over another, or one race over another. May unity be welded between them in the love of our beloved brother, Jesus, our teacher.*[4]

More recently, the seven Trappist monks of Tibhirine in Alge-ria, victims of terrorism in another civil war, foresaw their deaths as an offering for the country. The monks lived among their Mus-lim neighbors, not to convert them, but in friendship. They taught the impoverished villagers French, gave employment to some, and to others, clothes. One of the monks, a physician, provided medi-cal care. Because the terrorists targeted civilians, they had been warned to leave Algeria. After prayer and discussion, however, they decided to stay. At 1:45 in the morning of March 27, 1996, guer-rillas from the GIA (Armed Islamic Group) entered the monastery and kidnapped the seven monks whom they found there; two monks remained undiscovered. Two months later, the decapitated heads of the seven monks were found. The circumstances of their deaths remain controversial. Though the guerrillas claimed responsibility for their deaths, others claim that the Algerian Army unknowingly killed the monks in a helicopter attack on the terrorist camp where they were being held.

Christian de Chergé, prior of the community, had anticipated their fate. Two years before their deaths, he drafted a spiritual testament, greeting "the friend of my final moment" and saying, "If it should happen one day…that I become a victim of the terrorism which now seems ready to engulf all the foreigners living in Algeria, I would like my community, my Church, my family to remember that my life was GIVEN to God and to this country." Their story is beautifully told in the film *Of Gods and Men* (2010).

We are all called upon to forgive others. We often carry memories of those who have wronged us, sometimes for years. Injuries or wounds suffered in our families are especially painful. They continue to divide. So also in the Church; we need to pray for the many victims of sexual abuse; for those bishops who have abused their power, thinking not of those who have suffered but only of protecting the Church's reputation, or, worse, were blinded by clericalism. We need to pray even for those offending priests, most now removed from ministry. As more reports on abuse of young people continue to surface in different countries, we need to pray for the Church itself, and pray to be able to forgive it. As Fr. Don Farnan says, "The Church is not the only organism with negative subcultures within its structures."[5] And often we need to forgive ourselves.

But forgiveness is never simple or easy. As one of our graduate students, a young woman with three sons, once said to me that forgiveness is not given at once. It is a process and an attitude; it must be rooted in love. It loses its power when it blinds us to reality. I especially like that. Grace is all around us, but we cannot see it if we are blind to the real. Forgiveness does not mean ignoring suffering or evil or injustice. Forgiveness means being willing to extend a hand, to begin again and move on. Grace is often revealed in suffering, as in the broken body of Jesus, and in those who make God's grace visible to us.

In the early church of Rome, Christians gathered in the catacombs at the tombs of the martyrs to celebrate the Eucharist. They confessed their sins, asked the intercession of the saints, remembered their dead, and recognized the risen Jesus present among them. We do the same. At the beginning of the liturgy, we acknowledge that we are sinners and pray, "Lord, have mercy. Christ, have mercy. Lord, have mercy." And so we come to the altar of God, the God who welcomes, forgives, and transforms us, the God who gives joy to our youth.

While the contemporary Catholic liturgy, too often dismissed by arch-traditionalists as the *novus ordo* rite, is a vast improvement over the Tridentine ritual, both liturgically and theologically, it needs to be celebrated with care, reverence, and a conscious sense of the holy. The horizontal dimension should not overshadow the vertical. The Mass is so much more than a celebration of community. Too often our music sounds more secular than sacred. Is the piano the only liturgical instrument at our disposal? Do we draw on the riches of our liturgical tradition? There is a solemnity to the traditional Gregorian melodies and chants that can add depth to a service. Our liturgies should reflect both warmth and a sense of dignity. To enter the holy is to come into the presence of God.

When we go up to the altar of God, we come before him humbly, in prayer and adoration, to welcome Christ's presence in the gathered community and in the eucharistic gifts. We come to confess our failings and be transformed by grace. We come into the presence of the holy.

14

THE DARK NIGHT

SAINT JOHN OF THE CROSS was a short, slender friar, a member of the Carmelite order, recruited by Saint Teresa of Avila to join in her efforts to restore the order to its original spirit. John was born in 1542 as Juan de Yepes y Álvarez; his family, like Saint Teresa's, were descendants of *conversos*, Jews who had earlier converted to Christianity. He studied at a Jesuit college between 1559 and 1563, entering the Carmelite order in 1563, taking the name John of Saint Matthias. He then studied theology and philosophy at Salamanca. Blessed with a contemplative spirit, he had considered joining the Carthusians.

He met Teresa of Avila in 1567 at Medina del Campo. Teresa shared with the young friar her dream of founding a monastery of men who, like her sisters, would follow the primitive spirit of the order. When John consented, along with another considerably larger friar, Teresa returned to her sisters to announce, "Blessed be God, for I have found a friar and a half for the foundation of my monastery." John quickly became engaged in her movement, establishing with Teresa the Discalced (or shoeless) Carmelites, so-called because the friars and nuns in her movement went barefoot. On November 28, 1568, he founded the first house of the reform for men, changing his name to John of the Cross. The friars' way of life stressed daily Mass, chanting the hours, fasting, *lectio divina*, and solitude. In 1578, the community became independent, canonically separated from the rest of the order.

Not all the members of the larger Carmelite community appreciated the reform. In December 1577, some of them broke into the house in Avila where John was staying and took him captive to a monastery in Toledo where he remained a prisoner. Confined to a tiny cell, he was treated miserably, given public lashings before the community, and fed only bread and scraps of fish. During this time, he composed his *Spiritual Canticle* and probably the *Dark Night of the Soul*, considered today among the classics of Spanish literature. After eight months, he escaped.

Spiritual writers traditionally distinguish two different ways or paths in prayer. The cataphatic, or *via affirmativa*, appeals to our imagination, even our senses. It is exemplified particularly in the life of Saint Francis of Assisi. Francis found God preeminently in creation, in nature, art, the imaginative and affective. His love of the natural world, the animals and flowers of the field, art, and symbol all spoke to Francis of the divine. One thinks of his wonderful *Canticle of the Sun*, praising Brother Sun, Sister Moon and the stars, and our sustaining Mother Earth. Or the legend of Francis and the Wolf of Gubbio. When greeted by the saint as Brother Wolf, the wolf, who had been terrorizing the villagers, settled meekly at his feet and placed his paw in Francis's hand, to live afterward in peace with the people of the village. Among Francis's gifts to us is the Christmas creche.

Saint Ignatius of Loyola is also an example of the affirmative way. In his *Spiritual Exercises*, he placed great emphasis on praying with the imagination, calling on the retreatant to "contemplate" the different scenes from the Gospels. But Ignatian contemplation is highly imaginative; for example, in a contemplation on the incarnation, he encourages the retreatant to see the three divine persons looking down on the earth, seeing the variety of people, with so many being lost through sin, deciding "in their Eternity, that the Second Person should become man to save the human race." Then the retreatant should imagine the city of Nazareth and the house where Mary dwells. At times, he suggests putting oneself into the scene, even taking an active part. While there is sometimes a naïve dimension to some of these exercises, they are designed to make the gospel stories come alive for the retreatants, awakening their affectivity and touching their hearts.

Pope Francis also, with his Jesuit formation, is very much in this tradition, helping us to understand his appreciation of popular religion, with its local traditions, popular devotions, and religious images. Popular piety inculturates the faith; thus, Francis sees a value in "asking the saints to intercede, praying the Rosary, going on pilgrimages to shrines, reverently touching statues."[1]

The other tradition is the apophatic, the *via negativa*, which emphasizes silent, imageless prayer, a sense of darkness, even of God's absence, for the divine mystery lies beyond our ability to experience directly or even to understand fully. Examples are many. In the First Letter to Timothy, the author writes that God dwells in "unapproachable light" (1 Tim 6:16), Gregory of Nyssa spoke of a "luminous darkness," and Anselm of Canterbury echoed 1 Timothy in speaking of the "inaccessible light" that surrounds the divine. This tradition comes to expression in the pseudonymous author known as Pseudo-Dionysius the Areopagite (late fifth century) and in the great medieval text, *The Cloud of Unknowing*, a classic example. John of the Cross was very much in this dark tradition.

John's works, the poetic *Dark Night* and the more systematic *Ascent of Mount Carmel*, deeply influenced later spiritual writers, among them Edith Stein, Thomas Merton, Jacques Maritain, Hans

Urs von Balthasar, and Pope John Paul II. His famous poem, *The Dark Night of the Soul*, begins,

> On a dark night,
> Kindled in love with yearnings—oh, happy chance!—
> I went forth without being observed,
> My house being now at rest.
>
> In darkness and secure,
> By the secret ladder, disguised—oh, happy chance!—
> In darkness and in concealment,
> My house being now at rest.

The poet did not give this work a title. He speaks only of the dark night (*noche oscura*), his description of the soul's journey to union with God, and so the work is commonly known as *The Dark Night of the Soul*. The "house at rest" in the first verse refers, not to the stilling of worldly cares in general, but to the silencing of the body's faculties. Because God is transcendent, neither our senses nor our intellect can comprehend the divine mystery. Our senses find no objects, nothing to see, hear, taste, or smell, and so are frustrated; they remain in darkness. Neither can our intellect comprehend the divine; it reaches out, seeking to grasp and understand, but without success.

With our sensory and intellectual faculties deprived of their normal objects the experience can be painful, especially for those who so desire a sense of God's presence. This spiritual journey is one of purification, first of the senses and then of the intellect—the traditional three stages are purification, illumination, and union. Those new to prayer often experience consolation as they begin to seek God regularly, but as they continue, prayer becomes more difficult, drier, without sensible consolation. Many experience the dark night, people of great faith, saints even. In the last year and a half of her life Saint Thérèse of Lisieux, the Little Flower as she came to be known, longed for some sense of Jesus's presence and was troubled even by doubts about the God's existence, though she never gave in to them. The experience was painful to her; she told her fellow sisters that she was plunged into darkness.

So also Saint Teresa of Calcutta. When her letters to her spiritual director were compiled and published after her death, it was revealed that she had lived for years with spiritual dryness and emptiness in prayer, even with doubts like those of Thérèse of Lisieux. To her spiritual director she revealed what she called "the long darkness":

> So many unanswered questions live within me—I am afraid to uncover them—because of the blasphemy—If there be God—please forgive me....When I try to raise my thoughts to Heaven—there is such convicting emptiness that those very thoughts return like sharp knives & hurt my soul—Love—the word—it brings nothing. —I am told God loves me—yet the reality of darkness & coldness & emptiness is so great that nothing touches my soul. Before the work started—there was so much union—love—faith—trust—prayer—sacrifice.[2]

The British journalist Christopher Hitchens, one of the "new atheists," denounced her as "a fanatic, a fundamentalist, and a fraud," only giving evidence of his own lack of familiarity with the mystical tradition.

At different times in our lives, we may experience either tradition, the emptiness of the dark night or an overwhelming sense of God's presence. And there is no contradiction here. We confess theologically that God is both transcendent and immanent, beyond our ability to experience or comprehend and yet closer to us than we are to ourselves. We experience both.

In his later years, Karl Rahner spoke repeatedly of the incomprehensibility (*unbegreiflichkeit*) of God, something he learned from Thomas Aquinas, who taught that even in the beatific vision God would remain beyond our understanding. At the same time, Rahner said that the Christian of the future would be either a mystic or not a Christian at all. By this he was referring not to the extraordinary but to a genuine experience of God in our ordinary lives, sometimes recognized in moments of beauty, love, transparency, and hope, but also in those dark moments when God seems absent.[3]

When one is experiencing such interior darkness, the temptation is to give up and abandon prayer. But that would be to give in to what Saint Ignatius of Loyola calls desolation, those moments when the evil spirit tries to draw us away from God. Still, that temptation today is very real. In this secular age, we lack a Christian culture. There are few cultural supports to religious belief, and many people no longer practice their faith. With so much injustice, so much suffering, so much violence inflicted on the innocent, many, sensitive to these realities, find it impossible to believe in an all-powerful and merciful God. They ask: Is God there? Does God care? Does God hear my prayer?

These have always been questions for people of faith and especially for those who are suffering. And for those who care for them. These are real questions for many today. Even for religious people, as we have seen. A young Jesuit working as a chaplain at a grim jail for inner-city kids in Minneapolis was told by a guard that all of them would return, many to federal prisons. He wrote,

> Maybe if we all just believe in Jesus Christ enough he
> will blast through and save us. Like children at a "Peter
> Pan" matinee reviving Tinkerbell, if we keep clapping

and clapping and clapping our hands, Christ will appear and briskly lift us out of these tragedies. Is that how it is? Is it? An act of will can upend the whole rotten thing? Heresy, you say? Trying to force God onto the scene? Are we simply to wait? Wait to make sense of sadness, of evil? Then, as we wait, don't we begin to feel a little stupid?[4]

John of the Cross can be a help here. In his commentary on the dark night, *Ascent of Mount Carmel*, he counsels those experiencing the dark night to lean on faith even if it too seems dark, accept it for a guide and light, and rest on nothing that they understand, taste, feel, or imagine (2.4.2). "They must learn to abide in that quietude with a loving attentiveness to God. At this stage the faculties are at rest and do not work actively but passively, by receiving what God is effecting in them" (2.12.8). God comes in his time, not in ours. So we wait in a contemplative attentiveness to the God we know is there, united by an act of the will or, even more, by the desire of our hearts. Our hearts know what our reason often fails to grasp.

As a wise spiritual director once said, the most important thing about prayer is to just show up. God is indeed there.

15

SAINT PAUL

THE STORY OF SAINT PAUL is a stunning witness to the power of God's transforming grace. Born in Tarsus, a major trade center on the Mediterranean coast and named Saul after the first Israelite king, he tells us in an autobiographical passage that he was a Hebrew of Hebrew parents, of the tribe of Benjamin, and a Pharisee (see Phil 3:5). Paul's teacher was the famous rabbi Gamaliel, so he was well formed in the Jewish tradition; Luke quotes him to the effect that "I persecuted this Way up to the point of death by binding both men and women and putting them in prison," using the name, the Way, for the earliest Christian community (Acts 22:4). Luke also makes him a consenting witness to the death of Stephen, venerated as the first Christian martyr.

A difficult personality before his conversion, Paul must have been something of a fanatic, serious about his religious obligations, rigid in his observance. He was clearly intolerant of fellow Jews whose religious experience was different from his own, admitting that he was a "zealot" for his ancestral traditions, surpassing his fellows, even to the extent of persecuting the church of God and trying to destroy it (see Gal 1:13–14; Phil 1:6). His violence was most likely directed against the "Hellenist" or Greek-speaking Jewish

Christians like Stephen, Jews from the diaspora whose anti-Temple attitude was offensive to the more traditional Aramaic-speaking "Hebrew" Christians of Jerusalem who continued to take part in the Temple cult. As we learn from Acts, it was the Hellenist Jewish Christians who, driven out of Jerusalem after the death of Stephen, began the great missionary work for which Paul himself would be particularly remembered. He made three great missionary journeys to plant and care for churches that stretched from Jerusalem to Rome.

The story of Paul's conversion somewhere between the years 31 and 36, told twice in Acts, is quite dramatic (see Acts 9:1–22; 22:3–16). Paul, "breathing threats and murder against the disciples," is on his way to Damascus when a great light forces him to the ground and renders him blind, while the voice of Jesus calls out, "Saul, Saul, why are you persecuting me?" Led into the city by his companions, he is taken to a disciple by the name of Ananias who lays healing hands on him, restoring his sight, and then baptizes him. Rather than historical narratives, Luke's accounts are like the Easter appearance stories in the Gospels, designed to bring others to Easter faith.

Paul's own account is much more abbreviated. He says simply, "God, who had set me apart before I was born and called me through his grace, was pleased to reveal his Son to me, so that I might proclaim him among the Gentiles" (Gal 1:15–16), using the Greek *apokalypsai*, the verb for unveiling or revealing. In another testimony to the resurrection he says, "Last of all, as to one untimely born, he appeared also to me" (1 Cor 15:8). But little drama: no falling from his horse as in Caravaggio's dramatic painting, no details, only testimony to a revelation or appearance of the risen Jesus that was to change his life.

What has always been most impressive for me is the nature of that change. Paul, the zealous persecutor of his fellow Jews, the self-righteous Pharisee so anxious to justify himself by his perfect observance of the law became Paul the Apostle to the Gentiles, teaching that we are justified not by works of the law but by faith in Christ Jesus (see Gal 2:16). Henceforth, he was a different man, tireless in his efforts, rejoicing in "the freedom of the glory of the children of God" (Rom 8:21), in the freedom for which Christ has set us free (see Gal 5:1). His new sense of freedom, of grace, of the Spirit was to play a major role in the growth of the Church. His letters make up half of the New Testament, fourteen out of twenty-seven books, though some of them, called the Deutero-Pauline letters, were most probably written later by one or more of his disciples after his death, reflecting a different generation in the life of the early Church. They include 1 and 2 Timothy and Titus and most probably Ephesians and Colossians.

What was most important to Paul was his new relation to the person of Jesus, or, as he usually referred to him, Our Lord Jesus Christ, combining with the holy name of Jesus two important christological titles, Messiah and Lord. *Mašíah* in Hebrew, *khristós* in Greek, becomes Christ in English, literally "anointed one"; it refers to the expected Son of David who was to inherit an everlasting kingdom (see 2 Sam 7:14–16). Lord, *kurios*, was the Greek substitute in the Septuagint translation of the Hebrew Scriptures for the personal name of God, Yahweh, revealed to Moses at the burning bush. In his letters, Paul appeals repeatedly to his relationship with Jesus:

- For I decided to know nothing among you except Jesus Christ, and him crucified. (1 Cor 2:2)
- I can do all things through him who strengthens me. (Phil 4:13)
- I regard everything as a loss because of the surpassing value of knowing Christ Jesus my Lord. For his sake I have suffered the loss of all things, and I regard

them as rubbish, in order that I may gain Christ and
be found in him. (Phil 3:8–9)

- I want to know Christ and the power of his resurrection and the sharing of his sufferings by becoming
like him in his death. (Phil 3:10)

Paul's ministry was not without criticism. I am always encouraged to read of the difficulties that even this great apostle and evan-
gelist faced. Some opposed him, remembering his past persecution;
others, in the church at Corinth, continued to cause him problems.
The Christians there appear to have been a fractious group. His first
letter to the Corinthians found them divided into different factions.
Some were devoted to Paul himself, the community's founder, who
did not require Gentile converts to observe the Mosaic law but did
not prevent Jewish Christians from doing so. Some, most probably
more conservative Jewish Christians, saw themselves as followers
of Peter, or *Cephas* as Paul names him, using the Aramaic version
of his name. They would have been the traditionalist Jewish Christians, arguing for a more law-observant expression of Christian life.
Others, more culturally sophisticated, were followers of Apollos,
an Alexandrian Jew and skilled polemicist, known for his eloquence
in preaching and knowledge of the Scriptures.

Finally, there was the mysterious "Christ" party. Many scholars today see them as a gnostic group within the community who
thought of themselves as spiritually perfect, and therefore above
the law. It was probably this group that threw back at Paul his own
principle of Christian freedom to justify their lack of restraint in
sexual matters (see 1 Cor 6:12–20). Paul's response was not a
heavy-handed exercise of authority but a call back to unity in the
Body of Christ. He himself, despite his independence as an apostle,
was careful to maintain communion with the leaders in Jerusalem

(see Gal 2:1–10) and continued to support the Jerusalem church both materially and financially.

The church of Corinth was still having unity problems toward the end of the century, as we know from 1 Clement, traditionally dated around the year 96 CE. The work is attributed to Clement I, a leader in the church of Rome, who takes the community to task for removing their presbyters from office, a leadership structure then emerging in many of the churches. The church at Antioch, another mixed congregation of Jewish and Gentile Christians, also struggled for unity, as we know from Paul's letter to the Galatians and from the Gospel of Matthew. What is of interest here is that problems of unity are nothing new in the Church's life; from churches in the New Testament to the Church today, the Church has struggled for unity, with differences and divisions, whether based on theological approaches, liturgical tastes, or ethnicity. The genius of Catholicism has always been holding unity and diversity together in one communion. In our own time, we have seen considerable opposition to Pope Francis on the part of a few, even some bishops.

Paul also receives criticism today for what some see as a patriarchal approach to women and their role in the Church. Certainly, Paul reflected the cultural values of his time. Still, I'm not sure this critique is always warranted. In his authentic letters, he is generally careful to address his remarks to both men and women, especially in his First Letter to the Corinthians. In a lengthy, rather complex section on marriage in chapter 7, he is careful to balance his remarks, saying a husband should fulfill his duty toward his wife, and the wife toward her husband, that neither has authority over their own body, which now belongs to their spouse, and that neither should separate or divorce.

In the case of mixed marriages, he says that if either has a partner who is an unbeliever, if he or she lives with that partner in peace, the unbelieving husband is made holy by his believing wife, and the unbelieving wife is made holy by her believing husband. Still expecting the imminent return of the Lord, Paul advises both men and women, husbands and wives, to remain as they are, either married or single, though recommending celibacy so that both may remain concerned about pleasing the Lord rather than pleasing their spouse.

The later "Deutero-Pauline" letters, written by a disciple of Paul when the Church was struggling to fit in to the patriarchal culture of the Roman Empire, suggest a different story. For example, in the First Letter to Timothy, forbidding women to teach or have authority over a man, we read, "Adam was not deceived, but the woman was deceived and became a transgressor" (2:14), a bogus exegesis attributed to Paul by the unknown author, an apostolic delegate working in the church at Ephesus. Some of the most offensive passages, telling wives to be submissive to the husbands and slaves to obey their masters, don't come from Paul himself but from Greco-Roman "household codes" (*Haustafeln*) or rules of domestic order, adopted as the early Church struggled to find a home in the culture of the Roman Empire (see Eph 5:22—6:9; Col 3:18—4:1; Titus 2:1–19; 1 Pet 2:13—3:7).

The First Letter to the Corinthians, an authentic letter, has some more problematic examples. Here we find the rule: "As in all the churches of the saints, women should be silent in the churches. For they are not permitted to speak, but should be subordinate, as the law also says. If there is anything they desire to know, let them ask their husbands at home. For it is shameful for a woman to speak in church" (1 Cor 14:34). Many scholars consider this passage a post-Pauline addition to the letter. A later passage asks that the women participating in worship at Corinth be veiled. It is an interesting passage. First, it indicates that women at Corinth were participating in worship without head-coverings. Second, some scholars argue that Paul asks that they follow the custom of being veiled (1 Cor

11:5–16), lest they be confused with the unveiled maenads, women followers of Dionysus in the ecstatic mystery cults. Paul can appeal only to custom for this reason.

In other letters, Paul frequently greets women among his coworkers, including Phoebe, whom he identifies as a minister (*diakonos*) of the church at Cenchreae (see Rom 16:1), probably a house church, and Andronicus and Junia, "prominent among the apostles" (Rom 16:7). Some scholars today see him naming Junia, a woman's name, as an apostle.

Paul's apostolic ministry was never easy. I find especially helpful the last part of his Second Letter to the Corinthians where he talks about his own experience, with a lengthy recital of all he has suffered in his apostolic labors: beatings and lashes, shipwrecks and imprisonments, and dangers from robbers and from his own brethren. He frequently experienced discouragement. Some at Corinth compared him to those he calls the "super apostles," those more charismatically gifted who taunted him for being unimpressive in his personal appearance but powerful in his letters.

He freely acknowledged his weakness, being untrained as a speaker, yet always confident of God's grace. Occasionally, he could become sarcastic, telling the Corinthians that being wise themselves and willing to tolerate fools, they might accept him in the same way. Or writing to the Galatians about those insisting on circumcision, he writes, "I wish those who unsettle you would castrate themselves!" (Gal 5:12).

In all this, we can see Paul as a model for ministry. He worked to keep his churches united in faith and life. He does not want to be a burden to them but only to build up their faith. He suffered discouragement and criticism but is patient and forgiving, feeling the daily pressure of his concern for all the churches. Acknowledging his weaknesses, he even boasts of them. He mentions suffering from a "thorn in the flesh," some temptation, disability, or handicap, without being specific, asking the Lord three times to free him. Instead, he hears the Lord saying to him, "My grace is sufficient for you, for power is made perfect in weakness" (2 Cor 12:9).

Thus, he concludes, "So, I will boast all the more gladly of my weaknesses, so that the power of Christ may dwell in me. Therefore I am content with weaknesses, insults, hardships, persecutions, and calamities for the sake of Christ; for whenever I am weak, then I am strong" (2 Cor 12:9–10). Paul saw his strength coming not from his natural gifts but from the Lord.

16

A NETWORK
OF PRAYER

IN THE LAST DISCOURSE in John's Gospel, Jesus reassures his disciples that he will not abandon them or leave them orphans. His words are reassuring, tender even. "Do not let your hearts be troubled. Believe in God, believe also in me. In my Father's house there are many dwelling places. If it were not so, would I have told you that I go to prepare a place for you? And if I go and prepare a place for you, I will come again and will take you to myself, so that where I am, there you may be also" (John 14:1–3). A few verses later he tells them, "I will see you again, and your hearts will rejoice, and no one will take your joy from you" (16:22).

The same tradition appears in the Synoptic Gospels, though expressed differently. In words, which scholars claim are authentic, but which did not become part of the Church's liturgical tradition like those spoken over the bread and the cup, Jesus says, "Truly I tell you, I will never again drink of the fruit of the vine until that day when I drink it new in the kingdom of God" (Mark 14:25). Jesus has faith that God will not abandon him; he seems to be promising the disciples a renewed fellowship on the other side of death: This is our Christian hope from a biblical perspective.

In his encyclical *Spe salvi* on the theological virtue of hope, Pope Benedict XVI sees a belief in certain Old Testament passages that communion with God is stronger than death. He finds them in the Psalms (16:9b–11; 73:24, 26), in the Wisdom literature (Wis 3:1–12), and in Daniel (12:2) and 2 Maccabees where the idea of the resurrection of the dead surfaces. This hope in a life beyond life has been at the heart of Christian hope since Jesus's resurrection. It was the good news around which the gospel tradition developed. But today that hope seems to have faded. Most of my students do not believe in the resurrection of the body, even though it's an article of the creed. For that matter, they're not that familiar with the creed either. What they believe, if anything, is a vague cultural idea that somehow the spirit lives on.

Benedict traces the gradual loss of Christian hope back to the foundations of modernity. With Francis Bacon and the development of the scientific method, reason and empirical investigation began to establish humanity's dominion over nature. Christian hope was replaced by the secular idea of progress, while the Enlightenment relegated Christian faith to the realm of the purely private, freeing reason from the authority of Scripture, hierarchy, and Church.

Karl Marx was the fruit of this development. Benedict is surprisingly respectful of Marx, whose analysis of social injustice he does not contest. But he argues that Marx forgot that replacing the ruling class would not lead to the "New Jerusalem," for human freedom remains always freedom for evil and needs to be redeemed. To make his point, he turns to Theodor Adorno of the Neo-Marxist Frankfurt School, who argues chillingly that technical progress without ethical formation and moral growth has led only "from the sling shot to the atomic bomb." Seeing the reign of God as a creation of man, not God, Benedict argues, would only turn man against himself, something to which the twentieth century and the beginning of the twenty-first give tragic witness, with the millions of victims of Soviet Communism, Nazism, and other totalitarian experiments in social engineering. Nor have such efforts ended in the twenty-first century. Putin's war against Ukraine may be the latest example.

A faith, now privatized, also has a religious expression. Too many evangelicals have substituted an individualistic idea of "eternal life" for the rich biblical view of salvation, reducing the gospel to "getting saved" or "being born again" or "accepting Jesus as my personal Lord and savior." Some fundamentalists look forward to the rapture of the righteous (see 1 Thess 4:17), leaving the world and its people to its fate. Others preach the Prosperity Gospel, promising worldly benefits to those who join their communities.

But Benedict is insistent that what has been lost with this "thin" view is the rich patristic view of salvation as a social reality. Salvation cannot be understood individualistically; it always involves being linked to a lived union with a "people," with others. This means each of us needs to escape from the prison of our "I," finding salvation and life within this "we" that opens us to others and ultimately to God (*Spe salvi* 14). Francis stresses this in *Laudato si'*, arguing that we grow, mature, and become holy only as we enter communion with God, each other, and creation itself (*LS* 240), as we have seen earlier.

We use "heaven" as a symbol for a life beyond death but also for so much more. In the Old Testament, hope meant the triumph of God's justice, that God does indeed hear the cry of the poor, that all the victims of history will find recompense. In the Beatitudes, Jesus promised the kingdom of heaven to those persecuted for the sake of righteousness. The Book of Revelation tells us that every tear will be wiped away. Evil does not have the last word. We continue to witness to the kingdom in our ministry, in our efforts for social justice, in striving to respect our fragile home, "Our Sister, Mother Earth" as Pope Francis calls her, and in our prayer.

A fundamental principle of Catholic social teaching is a concern for the common good. But in the West, at least, modern individualism and social isolation make a case for the common good difficult to communicate. In the United States, Christian life must address the concerns of the many who do not share in the prosperity of the few; the needs of immigrants fleeing crushing poverty, violence, and the lack of employment; the scourge of systemic racism that continues to afflict Blacks and other people of color with its presumption of white supremacy; and the continuing degradation of our planet and its multiple life forms. We can help one another come to realize this if we take to heart the words Pope Paul VI, who wrote in his great apostolic exhortation on evangelization, *Evangelii nuntiandi*: "Modern man listens more willingly to witnesses than to teachers, and if he does listen to teachers, it is because they are witnesses" (no. 41).

Even those who live the monastic life share in this social view of salvation. Pope Benedict noted that those who entered the monasteries of Europe in the Middle Ages were not fleeing the world to seek their personal salvation. He cites Bernard of Clairvaux, the great early Cistercian, who said, "Monks perform a task for the whole Church and hence also for the world." He uses many images to illustrate the responsibility that monks have toward the entire Body of the Church, and indeed toward humanity; he applies to them the words of Pseudo-Rufinus: "The human race lives thanks to a few; were it not for them, the world would perish." Saint Thomas More had a similar view; when Henry VIII closed the monasteries, he exclaimed, "But who will pray for the dead."

Thus, salvation is not an individualistic reality; we are saved as a "we." Relationality is the key; we cannot be saved all by ourselves.

This participation or sharing in a common life is expressed by the Greek *koinōnia*, translated as fellowship or, better, communion. Paul continues to emphasize our union in Christ and with one another. He tells us that God calls us to fellowship with his Son, Jesus Christ (see 1 Cor 1:9). As disciples of Jesus, we are united by baptism into one Body and given to drink of one Spirit (see 1 Cor 12:13). We have a participation or communion (*koinonia*) in the body and blood of Christ, uniting us as his one Body (see 1 Cor 10:16–17), and he concludes his Second Letter to the Corinthians with a threefold blessing: "The grace of the Lord Jesus Christ, the love of God, and the communion [*koinonia*] of the Holy Spirit be with all of you" (2 Cor 13:13). For Paul, to be "in Christ" is always to be in his Body, the Church. One finds a similar expression of our horizontal and vertical communion at the beginning of the First Letter of John (see 1 John 1:3).

We are also united with those who have gone before us. The doctrine of the communion of saints means that we are in communion with the faithful of every age, grounding the practice of venerating Mary and the saints and invoking their intercession. The Catholic practice of praying for the dead is also an expression of the social nature of salvation. We find it in the late Old Testament (see 2 Macc 12:45), and it was affirmed by the Second Council of Lyons (1274). In his encyclical *Spe salvi*, Pope Benedict XVI writes that love can reach into the afterlife. Our lives are linked together:

No one lives alone. No one sins alone. No one is saved alone. The lives of others continually spill over into mine: in what I think, say, do and achieve. And conversely, my life spills over into that of others: for better and for worse. So my prayer for another is not something extraneous to

that person, something external, not even after death.
(*Spe salvi* 48)

We are joined in communion.

Salvation always involves the restoration of unity; it means overcoming the divisions symbolized by the story of the tower of Babel, the exclusion caused by prejudice, the alienation that results from sin. We join in the Eucharist, remembering Christ's sacrifice and commemorating the faithful departed. We pray the Prayer of the Church, linking us with others in reciting the psalms. In the Morning Offering, we offer up our days, our diminishments, our sufferings. In sharing our faith with others, we become teachers and witnesses. We are part of the Body of Christ, a vast network of prayer and communion.

PART IV

DISCIPLESHIP

17

VOCATION

GOD'S CALL IS A MYSTERY, but it is constant. The Hebrew Scriptures represent the wonderful story of God choosing a people to be uniquely his own: "It was not because you were more numerous than any other people that the LORD set his heart on you and chose you—for you were the fewest of all peoples. It was because the LORD loved you" (Deut 7:7–8).

The epigram "How odd of God to choose the Jews" has sometimes been attributed to Hilaire Belloc, though apparently it originated with the British journalist William Norman Ewer (1885–1975). But it represents what theologians call "the scandal of particularity" that is at the heart of the Judeo-Christian tradition, the idea that the transcendent God reached into space and time to disclose something of the divine mystery through the men and women he made particularly his own. Certainly, history owes the first revelation of that mystery to God's chosen people, the Jews. The Psalms, prayed daily by many Christians, help us to make our own their experience of a God who creates the heavens and the earth, who waters the earth to make it fruitful and feeds the beasts of the fields, who calls a people to himself and watches over them, filling them with joy and pardoning their sins. And though they have been persecuted throughout their history, diminished as a people, even marked for extermination by a godless, criminal regime, they continue to cherish that story and bear witness to that call.

Old Testament prophetic literature has many stories of God calling prophets to speak on his behalf. Some welcomed the call. Isaiah responded with enthusiasm: "Here am I; send me!" (Isa 6:8). Others were more hesitant, like Jeremiah, who protested, "Ah, LORD God! Truly I do not know how to speak, for I am only a boy" (Jer 1:6). Or Amos, who objected that he was just a country boy: "I am no prophet, nor a prophet's son; but I am a herdsman, and a dresser of sycamore trees" (Amos 7:14). Even Moses protested when God called him from the burning bush: "Who am I that I should go to Pharaoh, and bring the Israelites out of Egypt?" (Exod 3:11).

The mystery of God's choice continues into the ministry of Jesus and the New Testament. Jesus called certain men and women to join his movement. But the invitation was always personal; the disciple did not first choose the master; rather, Jesus chose and called his disciples; the initiative came from Jesus. He called his first disciples, Simon and Andrew, James and John, to leave their father and their fishing nets (see Mark 1:17–20) and Levi to leave his customs post to follow him (see Mark 2:14). From his disciples he chose the Twelve, sending them out to preach repentance, cure the sick, drive out evil spirits, and proclaim the nearness of the reign of God (see Mark 6:7–13; Luke 9:1–6; Matt 10:1–7). The Twelve, representing the twelve tribes of Israel, symbolized the renewed or expanded people of God, the Church. Later, Jesus appeared to Saul of Tarsus, a persecutor of the first Christians, calling him to be an apostle.

God's call often comes through our religious imagination. It is disclosed in our deepest desires and builds on our natural gifts. In his life of Saint Anthony, the father of monasticism, Athanasius's story of Anthony's call is classic. He describes Anthony shortly after the death of his parents, imagining the apostles leaving all their earthly possessions to follow Jesus, only to enter a church just as the story of Jesus's challenge to the rich man was being proclaimed: "Go, sell what you own, and give the money to the poor, and you will have treasure in heaven; then come, follow me" (Mark 10:21). Anthony went out, disposed of his inherited estate and his property, and, after providing for his sister, retired to the desert to a life of work and prayer.

The story of young Iñigo López de Loyola is similar. This proud hidalgo, the youngest of thirteen children, never saw himself as the founder of a religious order, let alone a saint. Born in 1491 into a Basque family of minor nobility, he became a page at the age of fifteen or sixteen in the service of a relative who was treasurer for the kingdom of Castile. With his imagination inflamed by tales of romantic chivalry, such as the Song of Roland, El Cid, and the Knights of the Round Table, he took up the life of a courtier. One of his friends said that, although Iñigo was attached to the faith, "his life was in no way conformed to it nor did he keep himself free from sin. Rather, he was particularly reckless in gambling, in his dealings with women, in quarrelling, and with the sword."[1]

At seventeen, he began a military career, continuing the rough ways of a man-at-arms. But that life shortly came to an end; he was badly injured at Pamplona in 1521 in a battle against the French when a cannon ball shattered one leg and injured the other. Brought back to the family castle at Loyola by his men, apparently helped by his erstwhile enemies who admired his courage, he endured three surgeries without anesthetic, including one in which he required the doctors to saw off a protruding bone in his leg that would have spoiled his appearance in the tights then fashionable.

During his long convalescence, desperate for something to read, he asked for the courtly romances he so enjoyed. However, his family estate had only two pious works, Ludolf of Saxony's *Life of Christ* and Jacobo de Voragine's *Golden Legend*, a popular collection of the lives of the saints. Reading these books changed his life, inflaming his imagination with thoughts of a life of another kind. He began to imagine imitating saints like Francis of Assisi and Dominic de Guzmán. By the time he was able to leave Loyola, with a limp that would mark him for the rest of his life, he was a changed man. Iñigo the courtier and man-at-arms had become Iñigo the pilgrim. His turning during his boredom to the life of Christ and the saints had opened his imagination, and indeed his heart, to the mystery of the divine.

In his famous autobiography, *The Seven Storey Mountain*, Thomas Merton tells a wonderful story of his own imagination moving him to a decision. Teaching at Franciscan Saint Bonaventure College in New York, he had sought entrance to the order but was turned down because of his past life, his wild days at Cambridge, which included fathering a child out of wedlock. As he tells us, he was walking the campus on a rainy evening, making a desperate prayer to find his way:

> Suddenly, as soon as I had made that prayer, I became aware of the wood, the trees, the dark hills, the wet night wind, and then, clearer than any of these obvious realities, in my imagination, I started to hear the great bell of Gethsemani ringing in the night—the bell in the big gray tower, ringing and ringing, as if it were just behind the first hill. The impression made me breathless, and I had to think twice to realize that it was only in my imagination that was I hearing the bell of the Trappist Abbey ringing in the dark. Yet, as I afterwards calculated, it was just about that time that the bell is rung every night for the Salve Regina, toward the end of Compline.

The bell seemed to be telling me where I belonged
—as if it were calling me home.

Whether this happened just as he described it or reflects more his literary art is impossible to determine. Nor does it really matter. What is clear is that God worked through his imagination, calling him to the monastic life for which we remember him.

Each of us has also been called to be in Jesus's company, to be a disciple. The author of the Letter to the Ephesians writes that God chose us in Christ "before the foundation of the world to be holy and blameless before him" (Eph 1:4). The stories of our own calls often remain mysterious, even to ourselves. Reflecting on where we have been touched by grace, how we have come to recognize God's call, what graced moments we have experienced can renew and deepen our faith.

Some of us were born into families that have been Christian for generations, a faith handed down by our ancestors or supported by our ethnic backgrounds or exemplified in the faithfulness and love of our parents. Some have stories of conversion, coming to faith by the example of others or in recognition of the good works of the Church. Some have been seekers, searching for a personal presence in the vast universe that often seems cold and impersonal. Saint Augustine was one of these. Others have opened themselves to God in times of personal tragedy or conflict, finding a sustaining presence. And as our lives unfold, we find that God's call is not a single event in the past, a discrete moment or "punctiliar" conversion when we got "saved," as some insist. For God is always present in our lives and continues to reach out to us, to call anew, to challenge us in moments that need to be discerned.

I remember one of those moments in my own life when I was struggling with the question of vocation, trying to decide whether I should enter the Jesuits. I had fears of not making the right decision, of entering and then having to leave, with consequent embarrassment. But one morning at an early Mass, the words of the Introit from the Gospel of John suddenly came alive for me. I read in my missal, "It was not you who chose me, but I who chose you and appointed you to go and bear fruit that will remain" (John 15:16, NABRE). It was as though God was calling me personally, summoning me to the Society of Jesus.

But that call is always an invitation, not a command. It often surfaces in our religious imagination. It is revealed in our deepest desires, in our true selves, not in our public personas. It is an appeal to our freedom that God always respects. Getting in touch with those desires is not always easy; it requires discernment, reflection, and prayer.

Nor is remaining faithful always easy. We live in a secular society, with little support for a life of faith. Many elites disparage belief, reducing it to superstition or an expression of fundamentalism. The Church itself is broken, damaged by the scandal of the sexual abuse of the young, or by clericalism, or by a lack of leadership.

Pope Francis is well-aware of the shortcomings of the Church, but still, he stresses the Church's mission. In his apostolic exhortation *Evangelii gaudium* (2013), outlining the program for his papacy, he says that all Christians are challenged to become missionary disciples in virtue of their baptism. Evangelization cannot be reduced to the work of professionals. All those who have encountered the saving love of God are called to be active agents of evangelization. Like the first disciples who joyfully proclaimed their personal encounter with Jesus to others, they share in the Church's evangelizing mission (*EG* 120–21). In a beautiful passage expressing his appreciation of "popular religion" he says,

> I think of the steadfast faith of those mothers tending
> their sick children who, though perhaps barely familiar

with the articles of the creed, cling to a rosary; or of all the hope poured into a candle lighted in a humble home with a prayer for help from Mary, or in the gaze of tender love directed to Christ crucified. No one who loves God's holy people will view these actions as the expression of a purely human search for the divine. They are the manifestation of a theological life nourished by the working of the Holy Spirit who has been poured into our hearts (cf. Rom 5:5). (*EG* 125)

Francis dreams of a "missionary option" that would move the Church from a focus on its own self-preservation to a transformative renewal of its structures, to make it more open and inclusive for the sake of its pastoral mission. This demands a renewal of our parishes to bring pastors and staff closer to the people, to better integrate small communities and movements with the pastoral activity of the local church, and to bring about a missionary conversion of the local churches themselves to enable them to bring the light of Christ wherever the need is greatest.

We each need to ask ourselves: Is Francis's vision of the Church the kind of Church we want? What does it mean for me to be a missionary disciple? How would I have to change? Where would my support come from, and how do I support others? For we too have been called to be missionary disciples.

18

BRIDGES NOT WALLS

MONSIGNOR HUGH O'FLAHERTY, an Irish priest assigned to the Roman Curia, is credited with saving some 6,500 persons, both Allied soldiers and Jews, from the German authorities in Rome during the Second World War. Protected by the Vatican's neutrality, he avoided various efforts by the SS to trap or assassinate him. After the armistice between Italy and the Allies in September 1943, with Italy still under German control, he used various disguises to hide his identity as he worked to find places in religious houses, convents, and the homes and farms of lay friends for Jews desperate to escape the Germans and for Allied POWs released from prison.

O'Flaherty's nemesis was Obersturmbannführer Herbert Kappler, head of the SS Sicherheitsdienst and the Gestapo in Rome. When Kappler learned that O'Flaherty was the person they were seeking, he ordered a white line to be painted on the pavement bordering St. Peter's Square, warning that O'Flaherty would be killed if he crossed it. Undeterred, the priest continued his efforts. By the time the Allies arrived in Rome in 1944, they found some 3,925 escapees aided by O'Flaherty's organization, including some Jews, all of them safe. But O'Flaherty also showed a concern for German prisoners of war, demanding that they be treated properly.

Having survived the war, Kappler was sentenced to life imprisonment in 1948 by the Italian government for having organized the Ardeatine Massacre that claimed the lives of 335 Italian civilians. The massacre was a reprisal for a partisan attack that killed thirty-three members of Rome's SS garrison. One of Kappler's few visitors in prison was O'Flaherty, who came monthly to discuss literature and religion with his former adversary. In 1959, O'Flaherty baptized him. Later, when terminally ill with cancer, Kappler escaped from the military hospital to which he had been transferred, helped by his wife, a former nurse whom he had married in prison in 1972. He died in West Germany in 1978.

The story of O'Flaherty and Kappler, a wonderful example of reconciliation, was portrayed in the 1983 TV drama, *The Scarlet and the Black*. This reconciliation between the Nazi officer and the priest anticipated a greater reconciliation between the Catholic Church and the Jewish community, long victimized by a supercessionist theology and the anti-Judaism, if not actual anti-Semitism, that had so long characterized Catholic-Jewish relations. It was not really addressed until the Second Vatican Council's decree, *Nostra aetate*.

In his Second Letter to the Corinthians, Saint Paul tells us that whoever is "in Christ" is a new creation, for the old things have passed away:

And all this is from God, who has reconciled us to himself through Christ and given us the ministry of reconciliation, namely, God was reconciling the world to himself in Christ, not counting their trespasses against them and entrusting to us the message of reconciliation. So we are ambassadors for Christ, as if God were appealing through

us. We implore you on behalf of Christ, be reconciled to
God. (2 Cor 5:18–20, NABRE)

The Church puts this passage before us on Ash Wednesday, inviting
us to seek reconciliation with our loving God and with one another.
Note here how the two are connected. This is not just a text for
Ash Wednesday; it should inform and transform our Christian lives.
God has reconciled us to himself, but we cannot truly be reconciled
to God if we are not reconciled to one another.

If the virulent anti-Semitism so violently carried out by the
Nazis has been conquered, anti-Semitism has not disappeared, and
racism still infects our society and culture, even if many refuse to
acknowledge it. People of color are especially affected. As Francis says
in *Fratelli tutti*, "Racism is a virus that quickly mutates and, instead
of disappearing, goes into hiding, and lurks in waiting" (no. 97). It
is a complex disease.

As Fr. Bryan Massingale argues in his book *Racial Justice and
the Catholic Church*,[1] the Catholic bishops in the United States have
written several pastoral letters on racism, though they have tended
to reduce it to personal attitudes and relationships, ignoring the fact
that the virus of racism lies much deeper in culturally embedded
structures of systemic racism and attitudes of white supremacy.

Bishop Mark Seitz of El Paso makes a similar argument. In his
hard-hitting pastoral letter, "Night Will Be No More," Bishop Seitz
acknowledges that words like *racism* and *white supremacy* make us
uncomfortable, yet he says that challenging them, whether in our
hearts or in society, is a Christian imperative. Citing Massingale,
Bishop Seitz says that racism is "really about advancing, shoring up,
and failing to oppose a system of white supremacy and advantage
based on skin color." Much of his letter is devoted to examples of
this system on our southern border, as he calls for our Catholic
community to become an "oasis of justice."

I know how difficult it is to address these issues in a homily. It takes a particular sensitivity to deal with them. Some are simply unaware of how much they have been affected by racial attitudes embedded in the culture. Others are unwilling to acknowledge them. The careless use of "trigger words" can easily occasion violent reactions. "Black Lives Matter" is meant not to suggest that other lives don't but to call attention to the many African Americans who have died at the hands of police officers. To many, "Critical Race Theory" sounds like one more leftist theory critical of our heritage, developed by elites in the academy, and some become enraged when schools include teaching about racial injustices in their curricula. I personally find it better to avoid the term. But we need to teach U.S. history honestly—the positive as well as the negative. Instances of racial prejudice and discrimination abound. Most of our children are ignorant of that history. We shouldn't avoid it because our children might "feel bad." Banning uncomfortable books is not the answer. We cannot sanitize our history to protect our children from unpleasant facts.

Slavery was legal in all the original thirteen colonies, though half of the states in this anticolonial experiment that became the United States had abolished it by the end of the Revolutionary War or the first decade of the nineteenth century. The founding fathers knew their new country would ultimately have to address the issue, but the union they were attempting to form was still too fragile. In the southern states, a considerable percentage of the population was constituted by enslaved people. At the beginning of the Civil War, there were nineteen free states and fifteen slave states. That war ended slavery at enormous cost to American lives, but the racist "Jim Crow" culture and segregation that followed, enforced by civil law and the Ku Klux Klan, endured for another hundred years. The Supreme Court was complicit in enforcing the doctrine of "separate but equal."

Indigenous American peoples or tribes also suffered from racist violence. Most were forced from their ancestral homes or slaughtered, not always in battle but deliberately by those taking their lands. For example, as recently as August 17, 2021, Colorado Governor Jared Polis rescinded an 1864 order by Colorado's second territorial governor, John Evans. That order called for residents of the territory to kill Native Americans and confiscate their land during a period when a flood of settlers was moving onto Indian lands, leading to violence between the two groups. One result was the Sand Creek massacre of November 1864 that resulted in the U.S. Army killing two hundred Arapaho and Cheyenne people, mostly the elderly, women, and children. Other examples include the Bear River Massacre of 1863, the Baker Massacre of 1870, and the Wounded Knee Massacre in 1890. In California, after the rest of his Yahi people were killed in the nineteenth-century genocide, Ishi, the last surviving member finally emerged from his isolation on Deer Creek in the Sierras at Oroville in 1911. He spent the last five years of his life living in a University of California building in San Francisco.[2]

Asian immigrants to the United States also suffered from discrimination and violence. After the work of so many Chinese immigrants in pushing the first transcontinental railroad through the Sierras at considerable cost, six years later the country began to enact laws banning immigration from China. The Page Act of 1875, introduced by California Republican Representative Horace F. Page, excluded Asian women "to end the danger of cheap Chinese labor and immoral Chinese women." In 1882, President Chester A. Arthur signed the Chinese Exclusion Act, barring Chinese men. With growing tension over immigration from Japan, the San Francisco Board of Education in 1906 required Japanese children to attend separate, segregated schools. President Theodore Roosevelt forced an end to the policy a year later, but restrictions on Asian immigration remained. Shamefully, some 120,000 people of Japanese ancestry living on the West coast, many of them American citizens, were placed in concentration camps during World War II.[3]

Many Americans are unaware of how many African Americans were victims of lynching over a period of some eighty years, though statistics vary. The Tuskegee Institute, considered the most complete record, reports that 3,743 African Americans and 1,297 whites were lynched between 1882 and 1968, though "whites" in this case includes Mexicans, Native Americans, and Chinese. The Equal Justice Initiative in Montgomery, Alabama, lists 3,959 victims of "racial terror lynchings" in Southern states between 1877 and 1950. Many of us remember the violence occasioned by the Civil Rights Movement, energized by the murder of Emmett Till in Mississippi in 1956 and Rosa Parks's refusal to give up her seat on a Montgomery bus for a white passenger in 1955.

From the beginning of his pontificate, Pope Francis has been concerned about overcoming the divisions between peoples today, between the wealthy and the very poor, between prosperous nations and desperate immigrants, between Christians and Muslims, between Christians divided by their ecclesial traditions. In his encyclical *Fratelli tutti*, Francis writes that God calls us to live as one human family. He says our sense of belonging to a single human family is fading, while the dream of working together for justice and peace seems an outdated utopia, replaced by a cool, comfortable, and globalized indifference (no. 30). We remain isolated from one another, cut off, in silos by ourselves, too often angry and disconnected. We need reconciliation, we need to discover one another as brothers and sisters.

After a visit to Morocco in March 2019, Francis spoke of the need to build bridges between Christians and Muslims, commenting that "we feel pain when we see persons that prefer to build walls. Why do we have pain? Because those who build walls end up being prisoners of the walls that they have built. However, those who build bridges go forward....To build bridges is for me something that almost goes beyond the human, it needs very great efforts."[4] Building a bridge is another way of talking about reconciliation. A bridge brings together people who have been separated. But crossing over is not always easy. Msgr. O'Flaherty built a bridge to his old enemy Kappler; perhaps he also opened him to God's saving grace.

19

CHANGE

CHANGE IS ALWAYS DIFFICULT. It means accepting different ways of doing things, opening ourselves to new possibilities, moving beyond deeply held convictions, changing our minds. It can be threatening, leaving behind the security of the familiar and venturing into the unknown. Many resist change at all costs. Logic, reason, facts, data, and science—none of this makes any difference if we are emotionally wedded to a particular viewpoint or customary way of doing things. Our subconscious generates spurious reasons of what might happen. We worry about losing control. We fall prey to conspiracy theories. But change is inescapably intrinsic to life, whether biological, political, emotional, or intellectual. It is unavoidable; to resist it is to close oneself in, to refuse to grow, to remain static or lifeless.

Even our religious traditions change and hopefully develop and deepen. If we are truly open, we continue to learn and to recognize where our ideas have fallen short. Our theological language can often be improved. We begin to see more deeply, reach higher viewpoints, and change. Institutions too can initiate changes, even the Church. But it is never easy. An institution that never changes is dead. Garry Wills once called change the Church's "dirty little secret."[1]

Change has always been part of the life of faith. Imagine how the first followers of Jesus, all Jews, felt as they began to realize that their faith, now called "Christian," was distinct from the Judaism that had formed them. Conflict over circumcision and the law brought on by the coming of the Gentiles, the *goyim*, was the first great struggle faced by the early Church (see Acts 15). The decision was not an easy one. The author of Luke and Acts gives it a positive spin, representing Peter as arguing against "placing on the neck of the disciples a yoke that neither our ancestors nor we have been able to bear" (Acts 15:10). The Council of Jerusalem worked out a compromise, exempting Gentile converts from the obligation of circumcision and the law but still requiring some kosher observances. Paul's churches continued to be troubled, however, by those more conservative Jewish Christians insisting on circumcision, sometimes referred to as the Judaizers. They visited his churches, demanding that Gentile converts submit to circumcision. Paul argued vehemently against this, holding up the freedom Christians enjoyed in Christ (see Gal 5:1–2).

For us, looking back over two millennia of Christianity, all this is obvious. But try to imagine what it must have meant to a first-century Jewish Christian, having to leave behind their religious identity and sense of who they were as belonging to a people. Circumcision was the sign of the covenant, making them unique, God's chosen. The Mosaic law was God's gift to Israel. To some it seemed like they were losing their faith.

Many Catholics had a similar reaction to Vatican II. The Council marked the first gathering of the Catholic Church as truly a world church, not just a church of Europe and North America. It taught that grace was abundant and not just in the Catholic Church. Some Catholics found this very difficult to accept. They had grown up to believe that the Catholic Church was the one, true church, and now they were being encouraged to recognize God's grace in other churches and the ecclesial reality of those communities. For some, this was too much; they ultimately broke communion with the Catholic Church and went into schism. Today, Christians are called to restore communion to the fractured Body of Christ and to find ways to live in harmony and mutual respect with other religions.

Similarly, in stressing the primacy of baptism and the universal call to holiness, the Council began a process of moving beyond a clerical, top-down understanding of the Church. The laity were called upon to take an active part in the Church's mission, moving beyond what someone once described as a "gas station concept of church," a place where you go to fill up, to get your sacraments and your Masses for the dead. Liturgical changes were difficult for others to accept. Give up the solemnity of the Latin liturgy? Make the Mass less mysterious? Recognize salvation "outside the Church"? Most, however, welcomed the changes.

Today, the reception of the Council is still ongoing. Pope Paul VI did his best to implement its decrees, but Popes John Paul II and Benedict XVI moved much more cautiously; they tended to recenter all decision-making in Rome, rather than finding new ways to implement the Council's emphasis on collegiality, the laity's share in the Church's mission, and granting more authority to local episcopal conferences.

Liturgical issues were especially sensitive. Pope Benedict XVI had given priests general permission to celebrate the Tridentine liturgy, using the missal of 1962, hoping to bring about reconciliation with Archbishop Lefebvre's schismatic Society of Saint Pius X and other traditionalists who rejected the Vatican II liturgy. He also expressed the hope that the traditional liturgy could serve to enrich the reformed one of Vatican II. So his intentions were positive, but the results were quite different.

Some began to speak of "a reform of the reform," though Pope Francis rejected this idea, stressing that "to speak of 'the reform of the reform' is an error!"[2] For others, the Tridentine liturgy became a symbol for traditionalists and too often a rallying point for those in opposition to Francis's teachings. Not a few traditionalists oppose his teaching on marriage and the family, calls for economic justice and ecological responsibility, liturgical reforms such as washing the feet of women at the Holy Thursday Mandatum, allowing for female acolytes, receiving communion in the hand, and Mass facing the people. For still others, the Tridentine liturgy became a symbol of a wider rejection of the Second Vatican Council and the changes it brought to Catholic life.

Finally, Francis felt he had to act. After consulting many bishops throughout the world during their *ad limina* visits, as well as the Congregation for the Doctrine of the Faith, he issued a *motu proprio*, *Traditionis custodes* (July 16, 2021), greatly restricting the general celebration of the Tridentine or "extraordinary form" of the liturgy.[3] In an accompanying letter, he noted sadly that the use of the Tridentine liturgy "is often characterized by a rejection not only of the liturgical reform, but of the Vatican Council II itself."[4] His action caused a firestorm of protests among traditionalists. Though their number is not large, their protest was fierce. One blogger called the pope's *motu proprio* "an atomic bomb against the faith…a declaration of total war."[5] Though some bishops continue to allow it, Francis's action was in the name of ecclesial unity.

Change is not just an issue for the Church. Most of us find it difficult. Jesus calls all to a new way of life, to a conversion that is ongoing. The Gospels use *metanoia*, though the English word *conversion* suggests a narrow, moralistic repenting of one's sin. *Metanoia* is a much more comprehensive term. It suggests a change of mind, of attitude, of heart, in other words, an integral conversion. But that is not easy for any of us, especially as we get older. Change is always unsettling. We tend to become comfortable with our ways of thinking, our attitudes, our practices.

We see many examples of conversion in Scripture. Mary of Magdala went from being a troubled woman to a close friend of Jesus, though the Gospels never identify her as a prostitute. Zacchaeus's encounter with Jesus led this tax collector to give away half of his possessions to the poor and repay anyone he had defrauded four times over. Simon Peter changed from being a boastful individual unaware of his own weakness to a leader of the primitive church and a martyr. The case of Saul of Tarsus is the most dramatic. This rigid Pharisee, desperate to justify himself and resorting to violence against those fellow Jews who followed Jesus, became Paul the "the Apostle of the Gentiles."

Bernard Lonergan has described conversion as an integral, multilevel reality. It affects our approach to the real, to our self-understanding, even to our affective or emotional life, though this last point he developed only later in his career. Conversion is a process; it takes place in steps, not all at once.[6]

An integral conversion is intellectual. It means being able to grow in our understanding, to learn. Our ideas can become frozen; we are suspicious of new data; afraid it might challenge long-held positions. We are reluctant to investigate or seek counsel. Often our intellectual commitments are rooted in self-interest, especially in the realm of politics or economics. During the Trump administration, millions fell under the spell of baseless conspiracy theories spread on social media by QAnon. Millions more accepted without evidence the "big lie" about a fraudulent election. An intellectual conversion demands more than a commonsense approach to reality, which itself is complex and multilayered. It involves being attentive; investigating, formulating, and testing hypotheses; and making judgments. This process can lead to deeper understandings, higher viewpoints, and change.

An integral conversion also has a moral dimension. It means moving from self-centeredness to an orientation toward others, a process through which we begin to develop a moral consciousness based on transcendental values of the true and the good. We need to base our decisions and actions not just on mere satisfaction of personal desire but on what is right and just. Though most have a basic sense that good is to be done and evil avoided, these impulses are easily ignored. Theology calls this original sin.

As developmental psychologists like Lawrence Kohlberg point out, moral consciousness is not simply a given but comes from a complex process of development, both intellectual and affective. We need to develop as moral persons. Are there areas in our lives that call for a change of sinful habits or destructive patterns of behavior? Do we ignore prejudicial attitudes toward others, whether based on race, religion, or difference of others? Are we honest and respectful in our dealings with others, or do we tear others down in our conversation, spreading gossip or rumor? Is personal integrity important to us? Are we honest with ourselves?

Religious conversion is usually understood as moving from one faith tradition or church to another. But in another sense, it concerns our basic orientation toward what is ultimate. Have we opened ourselves to the transcendent; to the true, the good, the beautiful; to values that go beyond the immediate and ultimately to the divine? Being Christian means far more than attending services and keeping the rules. A religious conversion means being open to grace, to the movement of God's Spirit deep within us. It often begins with the experience of being loved and loving others in return. Thus, we move from being isolated individuals to being-in-relation with others.

It can also mean being open to change in our religious practice, moving beyond a literalism that is closed to deeper understanding, or opening ourselves to the importance of science and scholarship in understanding our tradition. We have already seen this regarding the Second Vatican Council and its efforts to bring about what Pope John XXIII called an *aggiornamento*, a bringing up-to-date or renewal of the Church. His famous example was to go to the window and open it, letting in a little fresh air.

A genuine conversion or *metanoia* also addresses our affectivity, our emotional life. It means facing honestly our joys and sorrows, our fears and repressed images. It means opening the secret parts of our lives. We all carry deep within us painful memories of past injuries, hidden wounds, and offenses. Often there are people we are unable to forgive, even those within our own families. We exclude them from our affections, avoid them, or give them the silent treatment. Some memories limit our freedom; we cannot afford to let them surface.

We inherit much from a culture that can blind us. The deficits of that culture are generally invisible to white people. But occasionally they emerge into view, as they did on January 6, 2021. It was mostly white supporters of President Trump carrying flags of the Confederacy, flashing the symbols of white supremacy, even invoking the name of Jesus in their violence, and storming the Capitol Building to overturn a legitimate election, falsely declared fraudulent by the then-president.

In his encyclical *Laudato si'*, Pope Francis argues that the environmental crisis calls us to a profound interior conversion, an ecological conversion. We need "to become painfully aware, to dare to turn what is happening to the world into our own personal suffering and thus to discover what each of us can do about it" (*LS* 19). But such a conversion does not come easily. Some committed Christians tend to ridicule expressions of concern for the environment. Others are passive, not wanting to change their habits. The effects of our encounter with Jesus the Christ should become evident in our relationships with the world around us. "Living our vocation to be protectors of God's handiwork is essential to a life of virtue; it is not an optional or a secondary aspect of our Christian experience" (*LS* 217).

Francis warns against demanding absolute certainty in everything. An encounter with truth requires an openness to the Spirit, discernment, the ability to confront complex problems that cannot be resolved simply by citing some norm. Like John Henry Newman, he sees truth as lying beyond us. "Newman was convinced, as I am, that in embracing what often appear at first sight to be contradictory truths and trusting in the kindly light to lead us, we will eventually come to see the great truth that lies beyond us. I like to think that we do not possess the truth so much as the truth possesses us, constantly attracting us by means of beauty and goodness."[7]

So often our unwillingness to change is rooted in fear. But fear is the opposite of freedom. Saint Paul tells us that we have been set free by Christ, called to freedom (see Gal 5:1, 13), not for an arbitrary self-indulgence but to live in the Spirit, to allow Christ to live in us. Life in Christ means showing in our lives the fruits of the Spirit—love, joy, peace, patience, kindness, generosity, faithfulness, gentleness, self-control (see Gal 5:22–23). It often means learning to live with ambiguity.

Cardinal Newman once said, "To live is to change, and to be perfect is to have changed often." Quite often, change is the result of God's grace.

20

KINSHIP

F R. GREG BOYLE, nationally known for his work with young people involved in the gangs of East Los Angeles and founder of Homeboy Industries, often talks about kinship. For him, it means that we are related to one another and therefore have a responsibility to each other. He likes to quote Mother Teresa, who says, "The problem in the world is that we've forgotten that we belong to each other." Our troubled world will not improve until we learn that lesson.

The judgments we make keep us apart from each other; they separate us. Fr. Greg cites the parable of the prodigal son. "The father did not see 'sin'; he saw 'son.'" In one of his talks, he said that "kinship is about saying, 'We belong to each other: homeless, immigrant, gang member. There isn't anybody who doesn't belong,'" The solutions to the pressing issues we face today, he says, "just won't happen until you know that somebody sleeping under a bridge belongs to you, and a woman with her kids fleeing this or that from Central America belongs to you, [until] then nothing really gets changed."[1] We need to widen the circle, broaden the definition of who belongs, make sure that no one gets left outside.

His best-selling books strip away the tough exteriors, going beneath the tattoos worn by the kids from the gangs to find the loveable but wounded person within. His "homies" come from broken homes; an abusive, addictive, or absent parent; and violent neighborhoods with failing schools and no opportunities for decent employment. Growing up without love and self-respect, they are burdened with shame and a profound sense of alienation. But with a job and paycheck, treated with trust and respect, with unconditional love, they begin to see themselves as the person God created them to be and cherishes. As enemies are brought together in the Homeboy Bakery and work side by side, they become friends, breaking down the illusion of separateness to replace it with kinship. The stories Greg tells are heartbreaking. So many cut down in drive-by shootings, remnants of a past they had moved beyond. But others, now with an apartment, a wife and child, a job, and a whole new future are testimonies to the transformative power of a radical kinship.[2]

Kinship is more than a virtue; it is rooted in the order of the cosmos. Pope Francis has especially stressed how all things are interrelated, interconnected. He speaks of an "integral ecology," one involving the social world as well as the environmental. In his encyclical *Laudato si'*, he argues that the ecosystem embraces not just the natural world but the social and the material as well—the physical, chemical, and biological. He writes, "Time and space are not independent of one another, and not even atoms or subatomic particles can be considered in isolation" (*LS* 138). A basic principle is that the whole is greater than the part. Nature can no longer be regarded as something separate from us or as a mere setting in which we live. We are part of nature, included in it and thus in constant interaction with it. The environmental crisis is multidimensional; it affects nature and society, the social as well the environmental.

If all things are related, "then the health of a society's institutions has consequences for the environment and the quality of human life" (*LS* 142). When institutions are weakened or corrupted by injustice, greed, violence, or a lack of freedom, the quality of human life itself in families and civil society is injured. As the pope insists, "A true ecological approach *always* becomes a social approach; it must integrate questions of justice in debates on the environment, so as to hear *both the cry of the earth and the cry of the poor*" (*LS* 49). One could say that kinship binds human beings not just to one another but to all creation.

In his third encyclical, *Fratelli tutti* (2020), Francis seeks to move beyond barriers of nationality, color, or religion to focus on fraternity, our dream of belonging to a single human family. The encyclical reads like a catalogue and diagnosis of the pathologies of contemporary society. It is a challenging document. The global economy unifies the world but divides persons and nations: "We are more alone than ever in an increasingly massified world that promotes individual interests and weakens the communitarian dimension of life" (*LS* 12). A "throw-away" world sacrifices some, especially the poor, the disabled, and the unborn, for the ease of others. A profit-based economy increases wealth but also inequality, with new forms of poverty emerging. "While one part of humanity lives in opulence, another part sees its own dignity denied, scorned or trampled upon, and its fundamental rights discarded or violated" (*LS* 22).

The equal dignity of women is far from reflected in how our societies are organized, while millions of men, women, and children are forced to live in contemporary forms of slavery. Human trafficking is widespread. Other offenses against human dignity include war, terrorism, and racial or religious persecution, a kind of "third world war," though one fought piecemeal. Perhaps inspired by images of the thousands of refugees fleeing persecution, war, and natural disasters in dangerously overcrowded vessels or endless lines at closed borders, the pope reminds us, mixing metaphors, that we are all in the same boat or lack a shared road map. At the same time, the fact that all things are interconnected means that the COVID-19 pandemic of 2020 is not unrelated to our claims to be absolute masters of our own lives and of all that is, including our lifestyles, relationships, and the organization of our societies.

Francis remarks that some populist political regimes blocking migration are putting lives at risk; others use social media to encourage xenophobia and racism. His critique of social media is particularly interesting, noting that a "frenzy of texting" replaces the careful listening that alone can develop relationships and build bridges. Efforts to move beyond ourselves, our families, and toward communion, fraternity, toward one human family are frustrated by racism. He reminds us that the right to private property is not absolute; the earth's goods are intended for all, and "each country also belongs to the foreigner, inasmuch as a territory's goods must not be denied to a needy person coming from elsewhere" (*FT* 124).

His teaching on other contemporary issues includes a critique of contemporary populism as a closed rather than open concept, appealing only to certain, often ideological sectors of a population, and he encourages the renewal of international organizations like the United Nations and multilateral agreements. The traditional arguments for the so-called just war and the death penalty, he suggests, are no longer valid. More serious are extrajudicial killings, which he denounces as "homicides deliberately committed by certain states and by their agents" (*FT* 267). Finally, he calls for religious freedom for Christians in those countries where they are a minority, noting that Christians offer that freedom to non-Christians in countries where they themselves have minority status. What is needed is to build understanding and harmony between religions so that all might come to discover that as children of one God they are brothers and sisters. This is what kinship means.

Speaking personally, I was most moved when, in the pope's extended meditation on the good Samaritan, he notes that the two men who moved to the other side of the road, ignoring the victim of the robbers, were both religious people, indeed, "clergy"—a priest and a Levite. How many times have I done that myself? As he says, belief in God and worship of God is not enough to ensure that we are living in a way that is pleasing to God. We are called to daily conversion.

Perhaps nothing has made our interconnectedness more obvious than the COVID-19 pandemic. The often-lethal virus, spread through airborne droplets or "aerosols" and highly contagious, has broken down the personal sense of autonomy or individualism that so often prevents us from recognizing our kinship. Social relations touch our lives, for better or worse. At the same time, social interaction itself has become dangerous, increasing our isolation through the practice of social distancing. Failing to take these and other necessary safeguards has endangered others. The human cost has been high.

For many, the pandemic has uncovered the systemic inequalities in our societies. The tragic death of George Floyd under the knee of a police officer moved thousands to demonstrate, energizing the Black Lives Matter movement. Others would talk only about Antifa, violence, and property damage, though actual instances of violence were quite rare. According to a study by the Armed Conflict Location and Event Data Project, only 6 percent of demonstrations by Black Lives Matter in 2020 involved violence or property destruction, whether by demonstrators, counterdemonstrators, or police officers.[3]

The poor, living in overcrowded communities, and people of color have been especially affected during the COVID-19 pandemic; lacking adequate medical care, many already have health conditions. Health-care workers and those unable to work at home, such as those in law enforcement, clerks in grocery stores, transit workers, and others in regular contact with the public, were particularly at risk. Many of those infected died alone, isolated from family and friends.

The need for effective public health care became more obvious as the poor and people of color were left without resources. Many of those in low-paying jobs, unable to work at home, were forced to employment sites where they were unprotected. Many children, already computer literate, were able to cope with online classes. Others, less affluent, found the transition to virtual learning difficult, while being forced to attend school online denied them the normal process of socialization.

Some people were revealed as completely caught up in themselves. Others exhibited an offensive sense of entitlement, revealing the rampant individualism that so fractures our society. Branding the pandemic as a hoax or conspiracy, they refused to take normal precautions, to wear face masks or observe social distancing. Some shouted at shopkeepers or airline agents when asked to wear a mask, insisting that it is their right to decide whether to wear a mask or not, that it is a question of their freedom. Some men consider wearing a mask a sign of weakness. One man said he considered dying from the coronavirus preferable to "wearing a damn mask." Others refused to get vaccinated, endangering not just themselves but others, especially the health-care workers who had to care for them when they contracted the virus. In several surges, they filled hospitals to overflowing.

A disregard for scientific evidence surfaced repeatedly. Some dismiss as exaggerations statistics on victims or those who have died. Conservative pastors insisted on conducting church services, despite the advice of physicians to avoid large indoor gatherings. States where this happened frequently experienced a spike in COVID-19 infections and deaths. Some have challenged advice from scientists regarding how to contain the virus, abusing physicians and specialists, occasionally even with death threats. These are a few examples of a conduct that lacks any sense of solidarity, kinship, or any concern for the common good. In his recent book, *What It Means to Be Human*, O. Carter Snead calls such behavior "expressive individualism."

Snead, a professor at the University of Notre Dame and one of the world's leading experts on public bioethics, reflects on human nature as embodied, with the implication of our vulnerable, mutually dependent, and limited existence. He describes expressive individualism as a type of human identity or "anthropology," crediting Robert Neelly Bellah with coining the term. Expressive individualism takes each person to be an isolated and autonomous individual, moved by their will toward an identity based on what seems to be their own unique "truths," however transgressive. "Because this anthropology identifies the person with his will alone, it takes the mind to be the seat of personal identity and regards the body as a mere instrument to pursue the projects of the will." Human relationships are merely transactional, based on agreements for the mutual benefits of the parties involved, while each pursues their own individual goals. From this perspective, claims of obligations make little sense. Nor can expressive individualism make sense of our dependence on others, let alone give a consistent account of our obligations to others, including children, the disabled, and the elderly.

To counter this, Snead argues that, in virtue of our embodiment, we are made for friendship and love. He points to newborns as a pristine example of the fragility, dependence, and finitude of human life, arguing that the newborn has a claim on all of us, especially his or her parents, for support and care, regardless of any recompense. "Viewed through the lens of the anthropology of embodiment...all living members of the human family are worthy of care and protection, regardless of age, disability, cognitive capacity, dependence, and most of all, regardless of the opinions of others."[4]

This is also the argument of Pope Francis. In *Fratelli tutti*, he writes, "In today's world, the sense of belonging to a single human family is fading" (*FT* 30). Or to put it another way, his encyclical is a lesson on kinship. We are all connected to each other and therefore responsible for each other. We are one human family.

21

MARRIAGE AND RELATIONSHIPS

TWO TOPICS IN CHRISTIAN ethics touch us deeply: one is sexuality; the other is social justice. Often these topics are difficult to discuss, even within the privacy of our families. They generate too much emotion and divide us from each other. Many on the right take the Church's official teaching on sexuality as the word of God, while dismissing its social teachings, objecting that the Church is meddling in politics when it advocates for the rights of immigrants, or the environment, or integration, or when it speaks out against racism and white supremacy or military intrusions.

Those on the left too often consider the Church's teaching on birth control, divorce and remarriage, cohabitation outside of marriage, homosexuality, gender identity, and abortion (to a lesser extent) as hopelessly outdated, the product of frustrated celibates isolated from the lives of real people, but they welcome its social teaching as deeply rooted in the gospel.

The Church's teaching on marriage is rooted in the two Genesis creation stories. The first teaches that the man and woman are created together in equality and mutuality, fashioned in the image of God, male and female (see Gen 1:27). The second story sees the woman as taken from the rib of man, teaching that the man without the woman is incomplete. So the Lord God creates woman as a suitable partner, and the two of them, united in mutual attraction, become one flesh (see Gen 2:24).

Based on these stories, the Church teaches that God has created man and woman for each other in what its theology would later call the sacrament of marriage, a union in which each sanctifies the other and brings new life into the world. Pope Francis likes to describe sacramental marriage as an icon of God and God's love.[1] Most of us are grateful for how deeply we have been shaped by our parents, who not only gave us life and faith but also shaped us into the men and women we are today. This is certainly my own experience.

But the statistics regarding marriage today are troubling. In the United States, the number of Catholic marriages between 1970 and 2014 dropped from 420,000 to 154,000. While 25 to 28 percent of Catholic adults have been divorced (the lowest percentage of any Christian group), the number of those seeking annulments has dropped from a high of 72,308 in 1990 to 18,558 in 2014. This suggests that far fewer Catholics today are marrying in the Church or seeking annulments when their marriages fail.

Concerned for Christian marriage, shortly after his election to the Chair of Peter, Pope Francis summoned two special synods to address issues pertaining to family life: an Extraordinary General Assembly of the Synod of Bishops in 2014 and an Ordinary General Synod in 2015. In preparation, the synod's secretary general, Cardinal Lorenzo Baldisseri, sent a questionnaire to all the world's bishops, asking them to survey their people on questions such as divorce and remarriage, the rules for annulments, marriages not recognized by the Church, contraception, and how to minister to people in same-sex relations. Though only a third of dioceses made the questionnaire available to their members, this effort to seek input from the laity was unprecedented. And the results should not have been surprising. The survey indicated that "many Christians 'have difficulty' accepting church teaching on key issues such as birth control, divorce, homosexuality and cohabitation."[2] What the survey showed was a disconnect between official church teaching and how so many of the faithful actually live their lives.

As the synod opened, Francis asked the bishops and cardinals gathered to speak openly rather than worrying about what the pope might think. The discussions that followed were some of the most open since Vatican II, with some participants openly disagreeing with each other, others bringing the debate into the media. They discussed issues such as acknowledging the gifts of homosexuals and welcoming them and admitting some Catholics in second marriages to communion, even without an annulment, while others argued that this would represent a change in church doctrine.

In his post-synodal apostolic exhortation, Francis suggested in footnote 351 that some of those in second marriages without annulments, after consultation, prayer, and discernment, might decide in good conscience to approach the sacraments, including the Eucharist. This was not so different from the "internal forum" solution widely used by pastors to help those who, when trying to obtain an annulment, faced obstacles impossible to overcome.

Francis was not giving general permission to ignore the Church's laws, warning that it would be a mistake to conclude that any priest could simply grant an "exception" (*AL* 300). At the same time, from the beginning, he stressed that "not all discussions of doctrinal, moral or pastoral issues need to be settled by interventions of the magisterium" (*AL* 3). And Jesuit that he is, he repeatedly called attention to the importance of conscience, experience, and discernment. *Amoris laetitia* places considerable emphasis on experience, referring to it more than eighty times in the English translation, keeping with his principle that "realities are more important than ideas" (*EG* 231). Twelve times he refers to conscience, noting that the role of the Church was to form consciences, not replace them (*AL* 37), and some twenty-nine times he calls for discernment. For those in "irregular situations," those in civil marriages or simply cohabiting, especially those with children, he says that it is not enough simply to recite the law. What they need is pastoral care and accompaniment, citing the teaching of Pope John Paul II who reminded us of "the law of gradualness" (*AL* 295), echoing Francis's own principle that time is greater than space (*EG* 222).

Francis's teaching in *Amoris laetitia* generated considerable criticism from some already opposed to his ministry. Four cardinals, two of whom have since died, publicly accused the pope of confusing the faithful. If he meant to change church rules about the divorced and remarried receiving the sacraments or engaging in acts of sexual intimacy, they alleged, he would be changing church teaching about marriage, sexuality, and the nature of the sacraments.[3] EWTN, the late Mother Angelica's massive TV network, hosted Joseph Shaw, president of the Latin Mass Society in the UK, who signed a "formal correction" of the pope concerning his teachings on the possibility of admitting the divorced and remarried to communion.

While not against doctrine, Francis knows instinctively that what sustains a person's faith is not doctrine but an inculturated faith and a more personal, experiential knowledge of God, a God of mercy and compassion who loves us deeply. In this he is like the Spanish mystics who stressed experience, or Orthodox Christianity, which prizes ritual, symbol, and beauty above rational constructions. Furthermore, a pope can't change doctrine by himself. He can only clarify and teach what the Church believes.

What about those who don't "fit" into the Church's ideal of sacramental marriage, those who are single, whether by choice or circumstance, or those who are gay, lesbian, or transgender, or those in same-sex marriages. Francis called attention to the problems faced by single mothers with children, stressing their need for the Church's care (*AL* 49). He also warns that those who chose celibacy run the risk of it becoming a comfortable, independent single life rather than an eschatological sign of the risen Christ (*AL* 162).

The two synods discussed how the Church could better reach out to those who are gay, but those efforts also generated considerable controversy. Certainly, a change is taking place regarding popular attitudes toward gay people. Where once they were despised and persecuted, today in most Western countries civil laws have changed to protect their rights, though in other parts of the world those rights are not yet recognized. Most recognize that being gay is not a choice but an orientation, something hardwired into a person perhaps even before birth. Young Catholics who grow up with gay friends open and out from an early age, even in high school, find the Church's apparent unwillingness to accept them as deeply objectionable.

The Church continues to wrestle with this issue and the attitudes of many Catholics have already changed. Many bishops are sympathetic and try to be welcoming. Several German bishops have called for a change in the Church's teaching. Pope Francis has continually called for greater acceptance. When the question about gays was raised on a flight returning from a papal visit to Rio de Janeiro, he referred to the *Catechism of the Catholic Church*, affirming that "these people should be treated with delicacy and not be marginalized. I am glad that we are talking about 'homosexual people' because before all else comes the individual person in his wholeness and dignity. And people should not be defined only by their sexual tendencies: let us not forget that God loves all his creatures and we are destined to receive his infinite love."[4]

Francis has said on several occasions that he has no intention to change doctrine: his instinct is always to include. But we can change our own attitudes. This may well be Francis's intention. While advocates for a doctrinal change will be disappointed, as John Langan suggested, the pope is prodding the Church to reconsider what its "stance" toward homosexuality should be, rather than what it has been. He would like to encourage a more discerning, compassionate stance, a stance based not just on rationalist arguments but on personal experience.[5] One often suspects that those who are most outspoken against gay people have never had any gay friends or sometimes are in denial about their own homosexuality.

The Eucharist makes us one Body in Christ, one people. We are indeed one family, with our brother Jesus, and our one Father in heaven. We should be more ready to recognize our siblings.

22

DIMINISHMENTS

SHORTLY BEFORE HIS DEATH, Jesus says to his disciples, "Unless a grain of wheat falls into the earth and dies, it remains just a single grain; but if it dies, it bears much fruit. Those who love their life lose it, and those who hate their life in this world will keep it for eternal life" (John 12:24–25). This gospel saying reflects very much the pastoral language typical of Jesus's preaching. But it has parallels in other places, in the Synoptics, where Jesus says that if you want to be his disciple, you must deny yourself, take up your cross, and follow him (see Mark 8:34; Matt 16:24). Luke adds to this saying the word "daily" (Luke 9:23). Or again Mark: "For those who want to save their life will lose it, and those who lose their life for my sake, and for the sake of the gospel, will save it" (Mark 8:35).

This notion of life through death is at the heart of the paschal mystery. It finds expression in Paul saying, "Do you not know that all of us who have been baptized into Christ Jesus were baptized into his death? Therefore we have been buried with him by baptism into death, so that, just as Christ was raised from the dead by the glory of the Father, so we too might walk in newness of life" (Rom 6:3–5). Paul speaks here of our dying to sin, but in the next verse he reminds us that if we grow in union with him, even in our dying, we will also share with him in the resurrection. We don't like to talk much about death, and our youth-oriented culture goes out of its way to deny it. But death is all around us; we read about it every day. It is a reality that each of us must eventually face.

Teilhard de Chardin, in his wonderful book *The Divine Milieu*, presents a Christian spirituality in a decidedly modern perspective. He offers an extended meditation on life and death, reflecting first on what he calls the "divinization of our activities" and then the "divinization of our passivities." The first refers to consecrating all our active efforts and daily endeavors by offering them to the Lord. This is the spirituality of the active life. Many do this in praying the Morning Office at the beginning of each day.

In the second half of the book, he writes about "the divinization of our passivities." This section often touches us more deeply. His concern here is not what we do, our active life, but what we undergo or suffer, things over which we have no control. As someone who suffered considerably in his own life, Teilhard knows of what he speaks. He was misunderstood both by the Church and by the Society of Jesus during his lifetime, forbidden to publish much of his work, considered unorthodox or simply a dreamer. He died far from his home in France and was buried in New York.

In writing about the divinization of our passivities, he focuses on those things that befall us because of our faults, sins, or the changing circumstances of our lives. What he offers us is a spirituality for our seniority, for our old age, as we approach our own deaths. How can our very diminishments lead to a reconciliation with our failures and sufferings, to the transfiguration of our weakness, even to communion as we abandon ourselves to God's Providence?

We all experience diminishments as we age. Our energy level sags; we can't do things we used to take for granted. We start reducing our exercise routines, our walks, the tasks we take on each day. We find our energy level fades at midday or in the early afternoon;

we fall asleep over the newspaper. We take more naps, turn down invitations, find new ways to conserve our energy.

Our health too begins to decline. We have aches and pains in places hitherto unknown. Sore feet, back pains, stiff necks. We begin adding new doctors to visit, new "procedures" to undergo, new medications, till our medicine cabinets are overflowing with bottles. Or, as I like to say, as we get older, "Each year, another doctor and another pill."

And surgeries: knee and hip joints, heart, and prostate. Our minds are not as sharp as they once were or seem to move more slowly. I notice forgetting little routines or confusing them; I go out without my glasses, forget my jacket, lose things, and can't find them as easily. I search for my hearing aid only to discover that it's in my ear. The body too begins to sag. Our reactions are not as fast as they once were. We don't stand as straight, walk as fast, or hear as well. As one of my friends says, as we pass seventy, everything bodily goes south! Recently someone in my community gave me a birthday card that said, "Don't let anyone tell you that you are old; just let it go in one hearing-aid and out the other."

Sometimes our spirits sag as well. We experience a low-grade depression. At times, we begin to question our faith. Things don't seem as clear anymore; we wonder what we have accomplished and whether it has all been worthwhile. Will anyone remember us, miss us when we're gone?

Teilhard writes about these feelings, encouraging us to bring them to God in prayer:

> When the signs of age begin to mark my body (and sill more when they touch my mind); when the ill that is to diminish me or carry me off strikes from without or is born within me; when the painful movement comes in which I suddenly awaken to the fact that I am ill or

growing old; and above all at that last moment when I feel I am losing hold of myself and am absolutely passive within the hands of the great unknown forces that have formed me; in all those dark moments, O God, grant that I may understand that it is You (provided only that my faith is strong enough) who are painfully parting the fibers of my being in order to penetrate to the very marrow of my substance and bear me away within Yourself.[1]

Teilhard is not speaking of a false resignation; he says we have no right to regard the evil that comes through my own negligence or fault as being the touch of God; giving into it is not submitting to God's will. On the contrary, we need always to struggle against evil as part of our Christian life.

But his remark that God is "painfully parting the fibers of my being" refers to God's power transforming the diminishments that come from our corporeality and our sin, even our death, transforming our lives into his own. He writes,

Now the great victory of the Creator and Redeemer, in the Christian vision, is to have transformed what is in itself a universal power of diminishment and extinction into an essentially life-giving factor. God must, in some way or other, make room for Himself, hollowing us out and emptying us, if He is finally to penetrate into us.[2]

Jesus himself knows our pain and diminishments. He suffered betrayal by a friend, abandonment by those closest to him, mockery by others, and humiliation. So also, he shared in our death. But the good news is that his victory over the forces of sin and death is also ours. His whole life was lived in union with the God he called Abba, Father, and he died commending his spirit into God's hands. God did not abandon him. He raised him up to life, showing that God's love is stronger than death.

Our sufferings are rarely like those of Jesus. And yet each of us must one day follow a similar path as we approach our final days and the forces of diminishment part the fibers of our own being. And so will we experience the separation of our souls from our bodies.

As those days grow closer, as we enter our seniority, each of us can ask ourselves: How is God's slow work taking place in my life, in my body, in my spirit? Am I continuing to struggle against evil, in myself and in the world? Where have I experienced greater communion with the God who dwells with me and is taking me to himself? What diminishments trouble me the most? What are my sufferings? Can I find God in them?

Is God making room for himself in me, bringing about my transformation, the death that leads to life?

23

LOVE

WHEN I WAS A YOUNG JESUIT in the early 1960s, a new culture of protest was surfacing. We were in the middle of the Cold War. The lunch counter sit-ins and freedom marches of the Civil Rights Movement were revealing to all America for the first time the violence that enforced systemic racism in the deep South. And the war in Vietnam was beginning to heat up, already generating considerable protest on college campuses and the streets of our cities. We young Jesuits were not directly involved, removed from it all by the protective environment of our religious formation. But the poignant music of Joan Baez was bringing that world of protest into our enclosed scholasticate, opening us to another reality.

A beautiful young woman, daughter of a Mexican father and Scottish mother, Joan Baez was a chanteuse, a folk singer whose melodies and poetic lyrics enchanted us and opened us to another world. In this age before cassettes, compact discs, and portable media players, we listened endlessly to her albums on twelve-inch "long play" vinyl disks that spun at 33⅓ revolutions per minute. One of her songs, written originally by Bob Dylan, has long stayed with me. Its title, "Love Is Just a Four-Letter Word," haunted me. In it, the singer is listening to a friend with her infant child on her knee, talking to the child's father, telling him that love is just a four-letter word.

I'm sure you recognize the word. I won't repeat it. But you hear it everywhere today. One evening, surfing around the television offerings, I heard it on three different channels in a row. It's an ugly word, reducing love to the merely physical, to "hooking up," even to a violent act.

How different is God's love! God's love is intensely personal. He has known us from before we were born and shaped us in our mother's womb (see Jer 1:3; Isa 49:1, 5; Ps 139:13). Our Christian tradition has always seen those Old Testament verses describing God's love for his people Israel as applicable also to each of us. We too are his chosen. He has created and formed us, called us by name. This is the God who spreads out the heavens like a tent, who numbers the stars and calls each one by name, who waters the earth and gives drink to the beasts of the field, the God who has redeemed us and made us his own. And God loves us.

For Christians, God is not an impersonal lawgiver or a philosophical principle, a cosmic architect who sets the universe in motion and then lets it run like a clock according to its design. As the author of the Fourth Gospel insists, God is love itself, love become person. Pope Benedict XVI stresses this in his encyclical *Deus caritas est* (2005).[1] He writes that "God is the absolute and ultimate source of all being; but this universal principle of creation—the *Logos*, primordial reason—is at the same time a lover with all the passion of a true love" (no. 10). The universe is neither a product of blind forces, of chance, or of an impersonal first cause or lawgiver; it is a work of love, which implies a lover, a creative force that is Being itself, pure existence, and at the same time personal.

Nor does Benedict hesitate to see *eros* and *agape* as essentially related, rather than opposites, as they are so often characterized in traditional theology. He sees them as different aspects or dimensions of a single reality. *Eros* is that profound attraction or desire that draws one person to another, just as it draws the creature to the Creator. It is the energy that drives the universe. But *eros* needs to be purified; undisciplined, substituting purely physical desire for intimacy, it can exploit the other, ignoring our deepest capacity for love, self-giving, and union.

Rather than an expression of *agape*, it becomes merely biological.

Agape is used for the biblical notion of an unselfish love that seeks always the good of the beloved; it can involve renunciation, sacrifice, even the willingness to give up one's life for one's friend (see John 15:13). God's love is agapic, the love of a personal, self-emptying God who through the Word pours himself into space and time and through the Spirit into all living things, into our Church, and into our lives. Thus, in Christian theology, God's love is trinitarian, the originating Father; the creative, only begotten Son born of the Father before all ages; the life-giving Spirit that is the fruit of their love. Again, in trinitarian theology, God is Giver, Given, and Gift-ing.

This personal, tender love of God that reaches out to us and draws us back to union with the mystery of the divine is expressed in the Catholic devotion to the Sacred Heart of Jesus. Far from the lonely prisoner in the tabernacle, demanding reparation for our sins, the Sacred Heart symbolizes God's love become incarnate, embodied in the person of his Son. The love of God is embodied in the flesh of Jesus.

Our love can never approach the immeasurable love of God. And yet, with God's transforming grace, which is our very share in God's life, we can also become loving men and women. That is why our Catholic tradition sees Christian marriage as a sacrament, celebrating the holy, life-giving love of man and woman, husband and wife. That is why in our tradition the vulnerable, the abandoned, the unborn, the sick or the needy, the prisoner on death row hold pride of place. In part 2 of *Deus caritas est*, Benedict speaks of the Church as a "Community of Love," for love or charity is essential to the Church's mission (no. 32). Here Benedict sounds very much like Francis, who continues to insist that the Church is not an NGO. For both, love is what makes the Church the Church, modeling and channeling the love that flows from Christ.

In his encyclical *Laudato si'*, Francis sees the Church's eucharistic worship not just as a religious but as a cosmic force. It joins heaven and earth, embracing and penetrating all creation. "The world which came forth from God's hands returns to him in blessed and undivided adoration." Citing Pope Benedict, he says that in the bread of the Eucharist "creation is projected towards divinization, towards the holy wedding feast, towards unification with the Creator himself'" (*LS* 236). Celebrating the love and offering of Jesus for his own, the Eucharist makes creation itself holy, consecrating it, raising it up to God, suggesting that our beautiful Earth is to be included in God's plan of salvation.

To understand God as love is to recognize that God continues to pour himself into creation as goodness, truth, and beauty. As the scholastics used to say: *bonum est sui diffusivum*, "goodness always tends to spread." We began this book with a reflection on God's creative work. That work is not finished; it is ongoing, a theme picked up by latter-day students of Teilhard de Chardin. John Haught writes about the hiddenness of God, who, from the future, yet present in each moment, draws the cosmos forward. This God suffers along with creation, revealing the divine suffering love.[2] He cites Karl Rahner, who speaks of God as the world's "Absolute Future."[3]

Ilia Delio, a Franciscan, finds Christ at the heart of the evolutionary process, bringing about unity "in the divine, continual act of creation, redemption, and sanctification of the total universe."[4] The marvelous, complex cosmos we inhabit is not the result of accidental combinations of atomic particles, nor is it some great machine of determined patterns and trajectories. It is God's work, the great drama of salvation in which creation and eschatology are correlative concepts.

But God is patient; the drama of life and of salvation is worked out slowly, not in moments but in eons. At its heart is God's Spirit.

NOTES

INTRODUCTION

1. See Francis A. Sullivan, *Salvation Outside the Church? Tracing the History of the Catholic Response* (Mahwah, NJ: Paulist Press, 1992).

2. Vincent J. Miller, "Synodality and the Sacramental Mission of the Church: The Struggle for Communion in a World Divided by Colonialism and Neoliberal Globalization," *Theological Studies* 83, no. 1 (2022): 11.

3. Michael J. O'Loughlin, "Most Young Catholics Say They Are Spiritual or Religious: That Doesn't Mean You'll Find Them at Mass," *America* online, February 24, 2022; see "The State of Religion & Young People 2021, Catholic Edition: Navigating Uncertainty," https://www.springtideresearch.org.

4. James L. Heft, *The Future of Catholic Higher Education* (New York: Oxford University Press, 2021), 194.

5. Massimo Borghesi, *Catholic Discordance: Neoconservatism vs. the Field Hospital Church of Pope Francis* (Collegeville, MN: Liturgical Press, 2021), 226–29.

6. Catholic News Agency, "Evangelization Must Start with Encountering Jesus, Pope Says," November 30, 2019.

CHAPTER 1

1. See Bill Bryson, *A Short History of Nearly Everything* (New York: Broadway Books, 2003), 23–28.

2. Thomas Aquinas, *De Potentia Dei*, q.1 a.1.

3. Bryson, *A Short History*, 342.

4. Elizabeth Johnson, *Ask the Beasts: Darwin and the God of Love* (London: Bloomsbury, 2014), 179.

CHAPTER 2

1. Daniel C. Dennett, *Darwin's Dangerous Idea: Evolution and the Meaning of Life* (New York: Simon & Schuster, 1995), 320.

2. See, e.g., Yuval Noah Harari, *Homo Deus: A Brief History of Tomorrow* (New York: Harper, 2017).

3. Flavius Josephus, *Antiquities of the Jews* 18.3.3.

4. See Michael Downey, *Altogether Gift: A Trinitarian Spirituality* (Maryknoll, NY: Orbis Books, 2000), 55–59.

CHAPTER 3

1. Antonio Spadaro, "A Big Heart Open to God: An Interview with Pope Francis," *America*, September 30, 2013.

2. Cited in Pope Francis, *The Name of God Is Mercy: A Conversation with Andrea Tornielli* (New York: Random House, 2016), xii.

3. Richard Leonard, *Where the Hell Is God?* (Mahwah, NJ: Paulist Press, 2010), xv.

4. Annie Dillard, *For the Time Being* (New York: Alfred A. Knopf, 1999), 167.

5. Jürgen Moltmann, *God in Creation* (San Francisco: Harper & Row, 1985), 88; see also David N. Power, *Love without Calculation: A Reflection on Divine Kenosis* (New York: Crossroad Publishing, 2005).

6. John Paul II, *Crossing the Threshold of Hope*, ed. Vittorio Messori (New York: Random House, 1994), 61.

7. Elizabeth A. Johnson, *Quest for the Living God: Mapping Frontiers in the Theology of God* (New York: Continuum, 2007), 193.

8. David Bentley Hart, *That All Shall Be Saved: Heaven, Hell, and Universal Salvation* (New Haven: Yale University Press, 2019).

CHAPTER 4

1. See Thomas P. Rausch, "Scripture, Tradition, and Church," in *Reconciling Faith and Reason* (Collegeville, MN: Liturgical Press, 2000), 53–70.

CHAPTER 5

1. Antonio Spadaro, "A Big Heart Open to God: An Interview with Pope Francis," *America*, September 30, 2013.

2. See Allan Figueroa Deck, *Francis, Bishop of Rome* (Mahwah, NJ: Paulist Press, 2016), 44–59.

3. "An Exclusive Essay by Pope Francis on a 'Personal Covid,' His Exile in Argentina," *America*, December 3, 2020.

4. See Massimo Borghesi, *Catholic Discordance: Neoconservatism vs. the Field Hospital Church of Pope Francis* (Collegeville, MN: Liturgical Press, 2021).

5. Antonio Spadaro, "'The Sovereignty of the People of God': The Pontiff Meets the Jesuits of Mozambique and Madagascar," *La Civilta Cattolica*, September 26, 2019.

6. "Letter of His Holiness Pope Francis to Cardinal Marc Ouellet, President of the Pontifical Commission for Latin America," March 19, 2016, https://www.vatican.va/content/francesco/en/letters/2016/documents/papa-francesco_20160319_pont-comm-america-latina.html.

7. Cited in Robert Mickens, "Time to Bury the Clergy-Centered Church," *La Croix International*, February 20, 2020.

8. Catholic World News, "In an Era of 'Epochal Change,' the Curia Must Change, Pope Says in Annual Address," December 23, 2019.

9. Pope Francis, "Visit to Lampedusa" Homily, July 8, 2013, https://www.vatican.va/content/francesco/en/homilies/2013/documents/papa-francesco_20130708_omelia-lampedusa.html.

10. See Massimo Faggioli, "Whose Rome? Burke, Bannon, and the Eternal City," *Commonweal*, October 18, 2018; see also Borghesi, *Catholic Discordance*, chap. 2.

CHAPTER 6

1. See Carl E. Olson, *Will Catholics Be Left Behind: A Critique of the Rapture and Today's Prophecy Preachers* (San Francisco: Ignatius Press, 2003).

2. Teilhard de Chardin, "Patient Trust," excerpted from Michael Harter, *Hearts on Fire: Praying with Jesuits* (Chicago, IL: Loyola Press, 2005).

CHAPTER 7

1. Michael Czerny and Christian Barone, *Siblings All, Signs of the Times: The Social Teaching of Pope Francis* (Maryknoll, NY: Orbis Books, 2022).

2. Cited by Peter Tyler, "A Contemplative in Action," *The Tablet*, January 1, 2022, 11.

3. Andrew M. Greeley, *Life for a Wanderer* (New York: Doubleday, 1969), 162.

CHAPTER 8

1. Taken from The Divine Office, Office of Readings for Holy Saturday, Second Reading: "From an Ancient Homily: The Lord Descends Into Hell."

2. Michel Downey, *The Depth of God's Reach: A Spirituality of Christ's Descent* (Maryknoll, NY: Orbis Books, 2018), 33.

3. Karl Rahner, *Foundations of Christian Faith: An Introduction to the Idea of Christianity* (New York: Seabury, 1978), 435.

4. John E. Thiel, *Icons of Hope: The "Last Things" in Catholic Imagination* (Notre Dame, IN: University of Notre Dame Press, 2013).

CHAPTER 9

1. John Paul II, *Crossing the Threshold of Hope*, ed. Vittorio Messori (New York: Random House, 1994), 61.

2. See Caroline Walker Bynum, *The Resurrection of the Body in Western Christianity* (New York: Columbia University Press, 1995).

3. Brian D. Robinette, *Grammars of Resurrection: A Christian Theology of Presence and Absence* (New York: Crossroad Publishing, 2009), 153.

4. See Neil Ormerod, "'And We Shall See Him Face to Face': A Trinitarian Analysis of the Beatific Vision," *Theological Studies* 82, no. 4 (2021): 646–62.

5. Joseph Ratzinger, *Eschatology: Death and Eternal Life*, trans. Michael Waldstein (Washington, DC: The Catholic University of America, 1988), 160.

CHAPTER 10

1. James F. Keenan, "Hierarchicalism," *Theological Studies* 83, no. 1 (2022): 84–108.

2. Sylvia Poggioli, "Morning Edition," National Public Radio, April 22, 2002.

3. Pope Francis, "Letter to the People of God," Vatican News, August 20, 2018, https://www.vaticannews.va/en/pope/news/2018-08/pope-francis-letter-people-of-god-sexual-abuse.html.

4. James F. Keenan, "Hierarchicalism," *Theological Studies* 83, no. 1 (2022): 105.

5. See Brevard S. Childs, *Biblical Theology in Crisis* (Philadelphia, PA: Westminster Press, 1970); also Sandra M. Schneiders, *The Revelatory Text: Interpreting the New Testament as Sacred Scripture* (Collegeville, MN: Liturgical Press, 1999), 22–23.

6. Andrew Greeley, *The Catholic Imagination* (Berkeley: University of California Press, 2000), 79.

7. See Paul Vallely, *Pope Francis: Untying the Knots* (New York: Bloomsbury, 2013), 135–41; also Austen Ivereigh, *The Great Reformer: Francis and the Making of a Radical Pope* (New York: Henry Holt and Company, 2014), 184–86.

8. Stephen J. Duffy, "Our Hearts of Darkness: Original Sin Revisited," *Theological Studies* 49, no. 4 (1988): 609.

CHAPTER 11

1. Gregory A. Smith, "Just One-Third of U.S. Catholics Agree with Their Church That Eucharist Is Body, Blood of Christ," Pew Research Center (July 5, 2019). Part of the present chapter appeared in my article, "What Do Catholics Mean When We Say That the Eucharist Is 'the True Body and Blood' of Christ," *America* online, November 12, 2021.

2. Paul Bradshaw and Maxwell Johnson, *The Eucharistic Liturgies: Their Evolution and Interpretation* (Collegeville, MN: Liturgical Press, 2012), 224.

3. David N. Power, *The Eucharistic Mystery: Revitalizing the Tradition* (New York: Crossroad Publishing, 1992), 244; DS 690.

4. Nathan Mitchell, "Who Is at the Table? Reclaiming the Real Presence," *Commonweal* 122 (January 27, 1995), 12.

CHAPTER 12

1. Hannah Brockhaus, "Pope Francis: The Cross Reminds Us of the Sacrifices of the Christian Life," Catholic News Agency, August 30, 2020.

2. See Peter J. Henriot et al., *Catholic Social Teaching: Our Best Kept Secret* (Maryknoll, NY: Orbis Books, 1988).

3. See Kevin F. Burke, *The Ground Beneath the Cross: The Theology of Ignacio Ellacuría* (Washington, DC: Georgetown University Press, 2000).

4. Pope Francis, in conversation with Austen Ivereigh, *Let Us Dream: The Path to a Better Future* (New York: Simon & Schuster, 2020), 120.

CHAPTER 13

1. See Justin Martyr, *First Apology*, chap. 65.

2. Waltraud Herbstrith, *Edith Stein: A Biography* (San Francisco: Ignatius Press, 1992), 180.

3. Anthony Bloom, "The Raising of Jairus' Daughter," homily of November 18, 1984, Metropolitan Anthony of Sourozh Archive.

4. Federico Lombardi, "Nicolas Kluiters: A Martyr for Faith, Justice and Peace," *La Civiltà Cattolica*, October 28, 2020.

5. Father Don Farnan, "Aberrant Subculture," Upon This Rock, blog, August 18, 2021, https://chargedwithstcharles.blog/2021/08/18/aberrant-subculture/.

CHAPTER 14

1. See Austen Ivereigh, *The Great Reformer: Francis and the Making of a Radical Pope* (New York: Henry Holt and Company, 2014), 182.

2. *Mother Teresa: Come Be My Light; The Private Writings of the Saint of Calcutta*, ed. Brian Kolodiejchuk (New York: Doubleday, 2007), 193.

3. See Patricia Carroll, "Moving Mysticism to the Centre: Karl Rahner (1904–1984)," *The Way* 43, no. 4 (October 2004): 41–52.

4. Joe Hoover, "Why Does God Allow Suffering: A Meditation," *America*, December 16, 2020.

CHAPTER 17

1. Cited by Philip Caraman, *Ignatius Loyola: A Biography of the Founder of the Jesuits* (San Francisco: Harper & Row, 1990), 13.

CHAPTER 18

1. Bryan Massingale, *Racial Justice and the Catholic Church* (Maryknoll, NY: Orbis Books, 2010).

2. See Theodora Kroeber, *Ishi in Two Worlds: A Biography of the Last Wild Indian in North America* (Berkeley: University of California Press, 1976).

3. Susan H. Kamei, *When Can We Go Back to America? Voices of Japanese American Incarceration during World War II* (New York: Simon & Schuster, 2021).

4. Gerald O'Connell, "Pope Francis: 'Build Bridges, not Walls,'" *America*, March 31, 2019.

CHAPTER 19

1. Garry Wills, *Bare Ruined Choirs: Doubt, Prophecy, and Radical Religion* (Garden City, NY: Doubleday, 1972), 21.

2. Gerald O'Connell, "Pope Francis: There Will Be No 'Reform of the Reform' of the Liturgy," *America*, December 6, 2016.

3. See Rita Ferrone, "Living Catholic Tradition," *Commonweal*, July 23, 2021.

4. Pope Francis, apostolic letter issued *motu proprio*, *Traditionis Custodes*.

5. Chico Harlan, "To Latin Mass Devotees, a Righteous Defiance," *The Washington Post*, September 19, 2021.

6. See Robert M. Doran, "What Does Bernard Lonergan Mean by 'Conversion'?"; https://loneranresource.com/media/pdf/lectures/What

%20Does%20Bernard%20Lonergan%20Mean%20by%20Conversion
.pdf.

7. Pope Francis, in conversation with Austin Ivereigh, *Let Us Dream: The Path to a Better Future* (New York: Simon & Schuster, 2020), 55–57.

CHAPTER 20

1. Dorany Pineda, "Father Greg Boyle Talks Hope, Homelessness and the Power of Kinship," *Los Angeles Times*, December 16, 2019.

2. See Gregory Boyle, *Tattoos on the Heart: The Power of Boundless Compassion* (New York: Free Press, 2010); also *Barking to the Choir: The Power of Radical Kinship* (New York: Simon & Schuster, 2017); and *The Whole Language: The Power of Extravagant Tenderness* (New York: Simon & Schuster, 2021).

3. Charles Homans, "Kyle Rittenhouse and the New Era of Political Violence," *The New York Times Magazine*, October 31, 2021, 29.

4. See Charles C. Camosy's interview, "Bioethics Must Recognize 'We Are Made for Love and Friendship,' Scholar Argues," *Crux*, October 21, 2020; see also O. Carter Snead, *What It Means to Be Human: The Case for the Body in Public Bioethics* (Cambridge, MA: Harvard University Press, 2021).

CHAPTER 21

1. See Pope Francis, *Amoris laetitia* 11, 29, 70, 121.

2. Josephine McKenna, "Vatican Confronts Shifting Landscape on Family Issues," *Religion News Service*, June 26, 2014.

3. See Edward Pentin, "Full Text and Explanatory Notes of Cardinals' Questions on '*Amoris Laetitia*,'" *National Catholic Register*, November 14, 2016.

4. Pope Francis, *The Name of God Is Mercy: A Conversation with Andrea Tornielli* (New York: Random House, 2016), 62.

5. See John P. Langan, "See the Person: Understanding Pope Francis' Statements on Homosexuality," *America*, February 25, 2014.

CHAPTER 22

1. Pierre Teilhard de Chardin, *The Divine Milieu* (New York: Harper & Row, 1960), 62.

2. Teilhard de Chardin, *The Divine Milieu*, 61.

CHAPTER 23

1. See Thomas P. Rausch, *Faith, Hope, and Charity: Benedict XVI on the Theological Virtues* (Mahwah, NJ: Paulist Press, 2015).

2. John F. Haught, *God after Darwin: A Theology of Evolution* (Boulder, CO: Westview Press, 2008), 54–60.

3. See John F. Haught, "Love, Hope, and the Cosmic Future," Center for Christogenesis, January 16, 2017, https://christogenesis.org/love-hope-cosmic-future/.

4. Ilia Delio, *Christ in Evolution* (Maryknoll, NY: Orbis Books, 2008), 132.